Also by Peggy Frezon:

Dieting with My Dog: One Busy Life, Two Full Figures… and Unconditional Love

Heart to Heart, Hand in Paw: How one Woman Finds Faith and Hope through the Healing Love of Animals

Praise for Dieting with my Dog
by Peggy Frezon

"Frezon tells a charming, true-life tale. * * * *" -*Newsday*

"*Dieting With My Dog* is sweet, funny, inspiring and adorable, just like Peggy and Kelly!" -Julie Klam, bestselling author *You Had Me at Woof,* and *Love at First Bark*

"Peggy's gracefully-told story of her shared journey to fitness with Kelly is a testament to the power of unconditional love." -*Dog Tipper.com*

"Humorous and very much recommended for pet lovers." -*Midwest Book Review*

"Peggy blends humor, candor and practicality in a wonderful way." -Julie Hadden, from NBC's "The Biggest Loser," author *Fat Chance, Losing the Weight, Gaining My Worth*

"Whether you're in tip top shape or looking to lose a few pounds, the book is a great read and engaging throughout." -*K9 Magazine*

"What I loved about the book was it just wasn't focused on weight loss – it also focused on the relationship and bond that we have with our dogs… There were several times I caught myself laughing and nodding my head as I read the book –it was so touching." -*The Philly Dog*

"A moving and instructive celebration of the bond between humans and animals." -Ptolemy Tompkins, author *The Divine Life of Animals*

"It's the story of how two buddies, Kelly and Peggy, stuck to their commitment to lose weight and change their lives for the better, together. I'm absolutely charmed by this book."-*Leland Dirks,* author *Angelo's Journey,* and *Seven Dogs in Heaven*

"With the book's rare combination of humor, practicality and inspiration, readers will become motivated to lose weight and gain a special bond with their dog." -*Linda Anderson,* co-founder *Angel Animals Network*

"The story reads like a good friend talking to you…" -*Pet News and Views*

"When you read *Dieting with My Dog*, you'll smile, be empowered to make healthier changes for yourself and your favorite pup, and feel like you've found a new friend in Peggy." -Dawn A. Marcus, M.D, author *Fit as Fido*

"Peggy is our hero, and Kelly is our mascot!" -*Shaggy Dog Stories*

The Dieting with my Dog Guide

to Weight Loss & Maintenance

How to get fit and healthy with your dog

The Dieting with my Dog Guide
to Weight Loss & Maintenance

How to get fit and healthy with your dog

Peggy Frezon

Published by H.S. Brooks Press

"The Doggy Diet" by Peggy Frezon from the December 2008 issue of *Guideposts* is reproduced with permission from *Guideposts* Magazine, Guideposts.org. Copyright ©2008 by Guideposts. All rights reserved.

"Doggone Excuses" by Peggy Frezon, from *Chicken Soup for the Soul, Shaping the New You, ©2010*

Any internet addresses (websites, blogs, etc) printed in this book are offered as a resource. They are not intended in any way to be an endorsement by the author or publisher, nor does publisher vouch for the content of these sites for the life of this book.

Copy editor and interior layout: Kate Fenner
Front and back cover photography and layout: Mike Frezon
Front cover design: Jodi Chick

Interior photos: Mike Frezon (pgs 2,11,14,15, 26, 34, 43, 46, 48, 50, 51, 73, 129-132), Donna B. Russell (pgs 16-19), Aaron Fenner (pg 25) Steve Pelletier (pgs 40, 42, 116, 120-122, 141, 142), Annette Vivian (pgs 52, 53, 55), Audrey Harvey (pg 57), Sarah Burdo (pgs 58-61), Jessica Rhae (pgs 62, 70-72), Kate Richards (pgs 64-67), Rosalyn Acero (pgs 68, 69, 77-79), Diane Silver (pgs 73, 75), Active Dog Photo (pg 74), Ellen Fay (pg 76), Michele Cuke (pgs 80, 84, 85, 119), Krista Wickens (pgs 81, 83), Tricia Montgomery (pgs 88, 91, 143), Liz Flowers (pgs 86, 87, 94-115, 144), Scott Nolen (pgs 92, 93), Patti Lawson (pgs 127, 128), Roy Gumpel (pg 149)

ISBN: 978-0615862064
Printed in the United States

Dedication

To Kate and Andy: my kids, my tech support, my friends.

Contents

IV. MAINTENANCE

V. RESOURCES

Preface

Dogs are good for our health. They can lower our blood pressure, predict seizures, aid mobility, increase immunities, and improve our mood.

And, dogs can help us lose weight.

A few years ago, my veterinarian pointed out that my spaniel-mix Kelly could stand to lose a few pounds. I didn't worry at first. I enjoyed making my dog happy with extra treats. The vet suggested that maybe I was making Kelly a bit too happy.

"Hmmm," she said, her hands pausing at a spot down Kelly's back.

"What is it?" I gasped. Was something wrong? Did she feel a tumor?

"Oh," the doctor said, "We call them love handles."

Seriously?

My dog wasn't obese. She was, however, chubby enough to produce deposits of excess fat on what should have been a shapely canine waistline. And the thing is, I had love handles too. My own doctor had been telling me for years that I needed to lose weight. I tried, although I never stuck to a diet for long.

But my dog…I'd promised to take care of her forever. So when the veterinarian told me that excess weight put her at risk for serious health concerns, I was determined to do whatever it took to help my dog slim down and stay healthy.

First, I decreased Kelly's feedings and learned everything I could about pet nutrition. Next, I set out to help her get more exercise. Kelly started to lose weight. Then, something extraordinary happened. *My dog* began motivating *me*. It was as if she was telling me to join her in these new, healthy efforts. Thus began our journey to lose weight and get fit together.

Often we'll do something positive for our much-loved pets that we wouldn't do for ourselves. But in this case, you don't have to choose. You can make your dog your diet partner. It's good for both of you.

Weight Loss

The Doggy Diet

Before: Kelly and Peggy with pounds to lose.

The numbers on the scale bounced up and down as my spaniel, Kelly, wiggled: 36, 34, 38…my eyes grew wide when the screen finally read 41. "She's up three pounds since her last visit," the vet said, turning to me and my husband, Mike. "For a small dog like her, that isn't good. It's like 15 pounds on a person."

"I'm feeding her less," I said.

"Are you measuring it?" the vet asked. She held up a small plastic cup and pointed to a line on it. "She should only get half a cup twice a day." Our scoop at home definitely held more than that. "And no table scraps," the vet continued.

Mike shot me a look. Just last night I'd given Kelly pizza crusts during dinner. "She shouldn't beg," Mike had scolded. I knew I shouldn't feed her from the table, but one look at her big brown pleading eyes and I'd given in. A little bit won't hurt her, I'd told myself.

The vet ran her stethoscope over Kelly's chest and abdomen. "If she doesn't lose weight, she'll be at risk for joint, skin and heart problems, even diabetes and cancer."

Wait. Hadn't I heard that before? Just a few weeks earlier my doctor had given me the same warnings. I weighed 171 pounds—way too much for my five-foot frame. Gyms, health books, diets—I'd tried them all. Nothing worked. Besides, I'd settled into a comfy routine. I worked from home, so during the day it was just Kelly and me. Only eight steps separated my office from the kitchen. How could I resist taking a break? I'd grab cookies for me and a treat for Kelly—she deserved it for keeping me company. And exercise? I sat at the computer while Kelly followed a patch of sunlight across the floor.

I looked at my chubby dog and the vet's concerned expression. It hit me: My bad habits were hurting Kelly.

It was the beginning of a new year. The perfect time for a change, for me and my dog. First, I tackled our eating habits. At lunchtime the next day I carefully measured a half cup of Kelly's food. It hardly filled the bottom of her bowl! *I've really been overfeeding her*, I thought guiltily. I looked from her bowl to my plate where I'd made a sandwich that was almost toppling over it was so laden with meat and cheese. I've been overfeeding myself too. I remade it with an ounce of turkey, a slice of low-fat cheese and a smear of mustard. I was surprised at how good it was.

By spring I'd learned to cook healthier. One night I was craving takeout. Instead, I made a salad with tomatoes from Mike's garden and skinless chicken breasts with green beans. "Delicious," Mike said.

I had to agree. But Kelly whined at my feet. "Can't I just give her a little treat?" I asked Mike. He shot me that look again, so I tossed Kelly a carrot. Not yet convinced, she hid it under the coffee table.

Both of us lost weight just by eating better. Now that the weather was nice, adding exercise was next. One May afternoon I finished work early. I looked at Kelly. She was sprawled on the back of the couch. "Time for a walk, girl," I called. Kelly barely raised her head. I tried again. "Let's go, Kel!" Kelly plodded toward me, stopping to stretch. I snapped on her leash. As soon as I opened the door the fresh air hit us. I took a deep breath. How invigorating! Kelly's nose lifted too. She swung her head and broke into a trot.

We walked farther than I thought we would—or could. "We'll get out every day," I promised. And we did, if it was sunny.

Then the rainy days piled up that fall. We returned to our sedentary ways…and the pounds stopped coming off. One day I glanced up from the computer and saw Kelly flopped on the couch, her big eyes sad. *Lord, Kelly trusts me and I've let her down. Myself too. Help me. Show me how to do the right thing for us.*

A few days later, I saw an ad for a used elliptical machine. I wasn't looking for one, but there it was as if it were looking for me. "What do you think?" I asked Mike.

"Great idea!" he said. "Put it in the living room." Perfect. On dismal days I'd hop on the elliptical and toss Kelly her ball. She'd run after it full tilt. Before long we were both full of energy. But it wasn't always easy. Once I pulled an all-nighter to meet a deadline. Tired and hungry, I went into the kitchen and opened the fridge. A friend had given Mike a chocolate cake; it sat there, frosting gleaming. I've exercised all week, I thought. *I deserve this.* But Kelly looked up at me with those big eyes. *Okay, Lord, I get it.* I grabbed a yogurt and gave Kelly a baby carrot. She flipped it in the air with her mouth and ate it.

Turns out Kelly and I make a great team. In just a year I lost 41 pounds and Kelly's at her goal weight, down six pounds. These days we have a new routine: I'll work for a few hours then march those eight steps into the kitchen. Only now I grab us both a nutritious snack. Kelly deserves a mom who will keep her healthy and stay healthy herself. That's the best trick this person learned from her dog.

After: Fit and healthy together!

 *YOU*

Health Risks from Being Overweight

About 60 percent of Americans are overweight or obese. We give in to decadent food and spend too much time in front of the television or computer, making it easier than ever to super-size ourselves. Because of this, we're increasing our risk for serious health disorders including:

- Diabetes

- Heart disease

- High blood pressure

- High cholesterol

- Respiratory problems, including sleep apnea

- Osteoarthritis

- Certain types of cancers

- Decreased life expectancy

YOUR DOG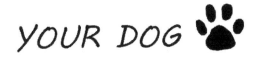

Health Risks from Being Overweight

Studies show that up to 54% of our dogs are overweight or obese. That's a lot of pudgy pups. By neglecting to manage our dogs' weights, we're putting our best friends at greater risk for[ii]:

- Diabetes

- Heart disease

- High blood pressure

- Skin problems

- Respiratory problems

- Osteoarthritis and other joint problems

- Certain types of cancer

- Decreased life expectancy

 *YOU*

Are You Overweight?

There's no one right weight for every person, just as there's no one right size for every breed of dog. Some people have larger builds, while others have smaller bone structure. But there are some ways to determine if you are in the appropriate weight range.

1. BMI or Body Mass Index[iii]

BMI is a numerical value of your weight in relation to your height. To calculate your BMI (you might want to get out your calculator for this):

Weight (pounds) ÷ [Height (inches) squared] x 703 = BMI

BMI less than 18.5= Underweight
BMI between 18.5 and 25 = Healthy weight
BMI between 25.1 and 29.9 = Overweight
BMI 30 or higher = Obese

If the math is making your head hurt, go ahead and use one of several online BMI calculators (see resource guide in back of book). BMI is not appropriate to assess your weight if you are under 20 years old, highly trained/athletic, pregnant or breastfeeding.

2. Waist circumference[iv]

The distance around your natural waist (just above your bellybutton) can help determine if you are overweight. According to the American Heart Association, if this measurement indicates that you are overweight, you may also have an increased risk of heart disease.

Women: Waist circumference of 35 inches or more= Overweight
Men: Waist circumference of 40 inches or more= Overweight

YOUR DOG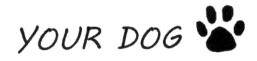

Are You Overweight?

Body Condition Scoring-[v] See which category best fits your dog.

Too thin		Ribs and spine are easily seen and felt. No indication of body fat. The dog looks bony and skeletal.
Underweight		Ribs, spine and other bones are easily felt. The dog has a defined waist and abdominal tuck.
Ideal body weight		Ribs and spine can be felt, with a slight layer of fat. There is a waist when viewed from above, and there is an abdominal tuck. The dog will look trim but not bony, and may be muscular.
Chubby		Ribs and spine are difficult to feel under a layer of fat. There is no defined waist or abdominal tuck. The stomach is round and full. The dog will have fat deposits on the hips and base of tail.
Obese		Ribs and spine are difficult to feel because of a thick layer of fat. There is no waist or abdominal tuck. The stomach is sagging. The dog will have plenty of fat deposits on the chest, back, hips, tale base and hindquarters. The dog will appear round and heavy.

*Chart based on information from Association for Pet Obesity Prevention.

 YOU

What Should You Weigh?

Use these charts to determine approximately how much you should weigh[vi]. These charts are calculated for adults wearing clothing and shoes with 1" heels.

WOMEN:

Height	Small Frame	Medium Frame	Large Frame
4'10"	102-111	109-121	118-131
4'11"	103-113	111-123	120-134
5'0"	104-115	113-126	122-137
5'1"	106-118	115-129	125-140
5'2"	108-121	118-132	128-143
5'3"	111-124	121-135	131-147
5'4"	114-127	124-138	134-151
5'5"	117-130	127-141	137-155
5'6"	120-133	130-144	140-159
5'7"	123-136	133-147	143-163
5'8"	126-139	136-150	146-167
5'9"	129-142	139-153	149-170
5'10"	132-145	142-156	152-173
5'11"	135-148	145-159	155-176
6'0"	138-151	148-162	158-179

MEN:

Height	Small Frame	Medium Frame	Large Frame
5' 2"	128-134	131-141	138-150
5' 3"	130-136	133-143	140-153
5" 4"	132-138	135-145	142-156
5' 5"	134-140	137-148	144-160
5' 6"	136-142	139-151	146-164
5' 7"	138-145	142-154	149-168
5' 8"	140-148	145-157	152-172
5' 9"	142-151	148-160	155-176
5' 10"	144-154	151-163	158-180
5' 11"	146-157	154-166	161-184
6' 0"	149-160	157-170	164-188
6' 1"	152-164	160-174	168-192
6' 2"	155-168	164-178	172-197
6' 3"	158-172	167-182	176-202
6' 4"	162-176	171-187	181-207

* Data from Halls.md and the Metropolitan Life tables.

Step on the scale with your diet buddy!

 *YOUR DOG*

What Should You Weigh?

Check out these weight ranges for various breeds of dogs.[vii] If you have a mixed breed, choose the most dominant breed and adjust up or down.

Breed	Ideal weight range (pounds)
Airedale Terrier	40-65
American Staffordshire Terrier	55-65
Australian Shepherd	40-65
Basset Hound	45-65
Beagle	18-30
Bernese Mountain Dog	85-110
Border Collie	27-45
Border Terrier	11-15
Boston Terrier	10-25
Boxer	50-75
Bulldog	40-50
Cardigan Welch Corgi	25-30
Cavalier King Charles Spaniel	10-18
Chihuahua	4-6
Chow Chow	45-70
Cocker Spaniel	23-28
Collie	50-70
Dachshund (Mini)	8–10
Dachshund (Standard)	10–12
Dalmatian	50–55
Doberman Pinscher	65–90
English Cocker Spaniel	26–34
English Setter	45–80
English Springer Spaniel	40–50
German Shepherd Dog	75–95

Golden Retriever	65–75
Great Dane	110–180
Great Pyrenees	85–100
Havanese	7–12
Irish Wolfhound	90–150
Labrador Retriever	65–80
Maltese	4–6
Mastiff	150–160
Newfoundland	100–150
Old English Sheepdog	60–100
Parson Russell Terrier (Jack Russell Terrier)	14–18
Pekingese (Standard)	8–10
Pomeranian	4–7
Poodle (Miniature)	11–17
Poodle (Standard)	45–65
Portuguese Water Dog	35–55
Pug	13–18
Rottweiler	70–135
Shetland Sheepdog	18–20
Shih Tzu	8–16
Saint Bernard	110–200
Toy Fox Terrier	4–7
Vizsla	45–60
Weimaraner	50–70
West Highland White Terrier	13–21
Yorkshire Terrier	Less than 7

Dog breeds that tend to be overweight[1]

*Labrador retrievers   *Dachshunds
*Cocker spaniels   *Beagles
*Shetland sheepdogs   *Basset hounds

 *YOU*

8 Tips for Getting Started in Weight Loss

You know what to do—eat less and exercise more, right? But we all know it's just not that simple. Beginning a weight loss program takes a lot of planning, determination and know-how.

1. Set attainable goals, and write them down.
2. Line up a great support system of family and friends.
3. Weigh in regularly and keep track of your weight.
4. Make one change at a time--such as drinking more water, skipping dessert, or cutting out late night snacks.
5. Make physical activity a part of your daily routine.
6. Start each day with a prayer, meditations or positive thoughts for your health and success.
7. Think positive.
8. Reward progress with non-food treats such as a manicure or time off to curl up with a good book.

* Always check with your physician before starting any weight loss program.

It's a good idea to stretch before and after a workout.

14

YOUR DOG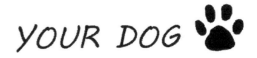

8 Tips for Getting Started in Weight Loss

Your dog can't manage its own diet and exercise routine, so it's up to you to make the necessary changes. Even better: doing it together!

1. Have your dog evaluated by your veterinarian. Decide together what and how much to feed your dog.
2. Commit to improving your dog's health and longevity.
3. Weigh your dog regularly. Most veterinarians welcome you to drop by and weigh in at no charge.
4. Understand food labels and invest in high quality dog food.
5. Make sure your dog gets plenty of exercise.
6. Make morning/nightly walks a habit.
7. If begging is a problem, keep your dog out of the dining room during your meal times.
8. Remember, *food is not love*. Love your dog with hugs, playtime, exercise and attention.

Chasing a ball is a great workout for Golden Retriever, Brooks.

The Perfect Diet Buddy

When Donna B. Russell realized she needed to lose weight, she never knew that the perfect partner was right at her feet. Now she's dieting with her dog, too!

When I was five years old, my father managed an ice cream stand, and my youngest brother and I enjoyed making our own treats. Also, my mother was an excellent cook. I loved her homemade pastries, donuts, and bread. Pizza and pasta were family favorites. So began my lifelong battle with weight gain.

Hard to resist: Donna's father managed an ice cream stand.

In addition to dieting, working out has always been a huge challenge. I've never been athletic—more of a bookworm with a sedentary lifestyle. After being diagnosed with fibromyalgia and arthritis, and experiencing the chronic pain and exhaustion that goes with them, exercising became extremely difficult, often impossible.

By the time I was 62, blood tests revealed that I was borderline diabetic. Though my blood pressure remained normal, my cholesterol and lipids were climbing out of the normal range. Excess weight, while not responsible for my pain, was a burden on my arthritic joints. Because I am gluten-intolerant, most diet foods were off-limits, making weight loss even more challenging.

Tired of diets that didn't yield lasting results, I decided to focus on living a healthier lifestyle: eating more fruits and vegetables, fewer processed carbs, and exercising as I was able, with weight loss as a side effect instead of the main goal. I joined an online weight loss program and began to lose, but still experienced some fluctuations on the scale.

Then, I adopted my dog, Paige. She came from an abusive breeding situation—no socialization, no proper nutrition or exercise, and no veterinary care. When we adopted her, she was a little underweight, though her tummy sagged from having had several litters. The vet wanted her to gain a bit, so we offered treats as rewards when housebreaking. Since she was highly food motivated, we also used liver treats and cheese during obedience and service dog training. At Paige's next checkup, she had indeed filled out, but too much!

Because I'm a bookworm, I turned to books to help, and discovered *Dieting with My Dog*. As I read it, something clicked. For the first time I thought, "This could actually be fun!" Here was someone who understood the frustration of emotional eating, and losing and regaining weight. Something else about the book intrigued me. Although I'd had weight-loss partners in the past, it had never occurred to me that my dog could fill that role. Looking at Paige, I thought, "Why not? If Peggy and Kelly could do it, so could we!"

I began substituting fresh fruits and vegetables for high calorie/high-carb treats. Instead of always using biscuits and liver treats as Paige's rewards, I substituted slices of fresh apple, orange and banana. We decreased her food to compensate for training treats, and used kibble in her puzzle ball about twice a week as a meal instead of a daily supplement. The puzzle ball encourages Paige to work off energy to get the food.

No longer a couch potato, Paige looks for opportunities to run outside.

For myself, I replaced most of my high calorie desserts with fruits, increased my overall intake of fruits and vegetables, decreased processed carbs, and kept a food journal. Now, one of my favorite snacks is an orange and a cup of green tea--satisfying, and nutritious!

With Paige as my diet buddy, playing together felt like fun instead of exercise. I increased her training activities and signed up for obedience classes through our local Humane Society. In addition to taking walks, Paige and I played fetch, tug-of-war, hide-and-seek, and did stair exercises. We also participated in an online pet fitness challenge in which weekly dog and pet-parent fitness activities were assigned, and participants blogged or posted comments about how the challenges were fulfilled. Paige and our cat Buddy also engage in rough-and-tumble exercise every day!

Because of all our work together, Paige lost her "mommy tummy," and regained her girlish figure. Her coat has improved, and she was given a clean bill of health by her vet. At her most recent check-up, I was concerned that Paige hadn't lost weight. However, the vet said it's because her muscle mass has increased. The goal now is for Paige to maintain.

As for myself, so far I've lost 26 lbs. The exciting difference is that this time I have kept it off for more than a year—something that has never happened before! At my most recent physical, my blood sugar, cholesterol, and lipids had all returned to normal levels. The doctor was very happy, and said to keep doing what I'm doing.

I no longer think of dieting, but living a healthy lifestyle—one that Paige and I can enjoy, hopefully, for a very long time.

-   Donna B. Russell

Paige gets some tips from a good book.

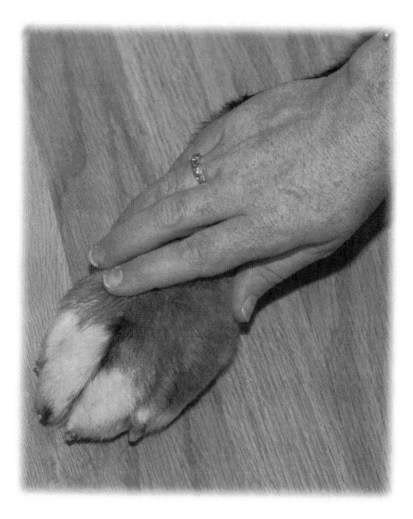

Everything's a little easier when you do it together.

Diet

 *YOU*

A Balanced Diet

My Plate

My Plate[viii] illustrates the USDA Guidelines that can help us make better food choices. Food is arranged on the plate in 5 categories— Protein, Grains, Vegetables, Fruits, and Dairy.

1. Half of the food on your plate should be fruits and vegetables.
2. Protein accounts for about ¼ of your meal.
3. Choose lean protein, such as lean beef, pork, chicken, turkey, beans, or tofu.
4. Choose mostly whole grains—such as whole wheat bread or brown rice.
5. A glass of fat-free or low-fat (1%) milk is a good option for your dairy.
6. The USDA recommends that you choose seafood as your protein source twice a week.
7. Choose high fiber foods, such as oatmeal, to fill you up.
8. Most of all, enjoy your food, but eat less.

YOUR DOG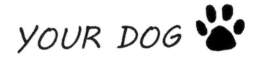

A Balanced Diet

My Dinner Dish

Dogs' nutritional needs are different than people's, but not everyone agrees on what's right to feed our pets. Along with your veterinarian or pet nutritionist, decide what is best for your dog.

1. Quality lean protein such as meat or poultry should make up at least 30% of your dog's food,[ix] and possibly much more.
2. Carbs can provide energy, fiber and a natural source of vitamins and minerals.
3. Corn is difficult to digest, and many dogs are allergic to corn and wheat. Grain-free diets are an option.
4. Fruits and vegetables are a natural source of vitamins and minerals.
5. Healthy fats and oils are part of a balanced diet. Home-cooked or prepared diets should include necessary supplements for a dog's nutritional needs.
6. Always provide plenty of fresh water for your dog.
7. Ask your veterinarian before offering your dog bones. Bones may cause broken teeth, or may splinter and cause punctures or choking.
8. If you feed commercial dog food, be sure to look for one stating that it adheres to the Association of American Feed Control Officers (AAFCO)[x] list of 37 nutrient requirements for dogs.

 *YOU*

Healthy Eating

The American Heart Association recommends that you eat a wide variety of nutritious foods daily.[xi] Most of us know that doesn't mean cookies and candy, and that we should opt for more salads and apples. Beyond this, however, how can we choose a healthy diet?

More Natural, Less Processed

Food in its most natural state typically is healthier for you than highly processed products. This is why nutritionists advise you to shop around the perimeter of the grocery store, where you find fruits, vegetables, poultry, meats, fish, and dairy.

Although you still have to be careful with your selections, it's hard to go too far astray with fruits and vegetables. One great tip is to make sure your diet contains fruits and vegetables of many different colors. This helps ensure a variety of vitamins and minerals (and it looks attractive too!). Limit starchy veggies such as potatoes and corn, and high calorie fruits such as bananas.

The USDA recommends 4 to 5 servings of fruits and veggies each day[xii]. This may sound daunting at first, but one example might be a cup of cantaloupe with your breakfast, lettuce and tomato on your sandwich at lunch, steamed green beans and a salad with dinner, and strawberries for dessert.

The Truth about Grains

It's easy to tell when apples and celery are in their natural state, but not so easy to determine if natural ingredients are included in some processed and baked goods. Does "enriched flour" sound healthy to you? It may sound superior, but actually enriched flour is farthest away from its most natural state. Enriched flour has been stripped of the grain's bran and germ[xiii].

Nutrients are added back in; however, they are not as healthy for you as natural whole grains which contain the natural bran, germ, and fiber. Bread labeled "multi grain" may contain many different grains, and "100% wheat" may be made with all wheat flour, but that doesn't necessarily mean that these breads are using the whole grain—meaning, the bran and germ. So, always look for whole grain in your breads, rice and cereal products.

Preparing meals from natural, less-processed foods instead of opting for boxed, frozen or convenience foods may take a bit longer, but it allows you to control the ingredients and make sure you are getting the most nutrition possible.

More Tips for a Healthy Diet:
*Limit saturated and trans-fats. Healthy fats include avocado, flaxseed, coconut oil, and olive oil.
*Limit sodium. Look for lower sodium versions soup, bread, frozen meals, and other food.
*Choose low-fat or fat-free dairy, and Greek style yogurt.
*Limit bad carbs and sugary foods. Try some healthy carbs such as buckwheat, chickpeas and quinoa.
*Limit added sugars. Naturally-occurring sugars are found in foods such as fruit and milk.

YOUR DOG

Healthy Eating

Pet experts have differing opinions about what to feed our dogs, but most agree that quality protein is a crucial component. Steve Pelletier is devoted to helping pets get fit and healthy. Through his studies on dog food ingredients, he has learned what makes a quality protein.

Nutritious food keeps Kelly lean and fit.

Protein in Dog Foods

In the health and fitness community, there's a dietary trend toward eating more foods that are closer to their natural state and fewer foods that are overly-processed or artificially-made. A good example of this is the Paleo Diet, which closely mimics the diet of the humans in the Paleolithic era (which ended about 10,000 years ago with the development of agriculture). It is essentially a hunter/gatherer diet consisting of animals and wild plants[xiv].

Although I am not "Paleo" with my eating, I do believe that humans should consume more foods that are found in nature and fewer foods that are highly-processed. I believe the same holds true

26

for dogs. If you feed your pet commercially-available dog foods, you should choose those with fewer processed and artificial ingredients.

Dogs are descendants of (a subspecies of) the gray wolf, a member of the Canidae family of the mammalian order Carnivora. Despite this lineage to carnivores, some people consider domestic dogs to be omnivores (consumers of meat and non-meat foods, like us humans). It is true that dogs can adapt to a wide-ranging diet, no doubt a result of them hanging around with us for the past 15,000 years or so. That said, I believe dogs should be fed a high protein diet and obtain a majority of their protein from real meat sources and not processed meats or non-meat sources.[xv]

Common Dog Food Proteins

Below, the Association of American Feed Control Officials (AAFCO)[xvi] defines some commonly used dog food proteins:

- **Beef** – the clean flesh derived from slaughtered cattle, and is limited to that part of the striate muscle which is skeletal or that which is found in the tongue, in the diaphragm, in the heart, or in the esophagus; with or without the accompanying and overlying fat and the portions of the skin, sinew, nerve and blood vessels which normally accompany the flesh.
- **Chicken** – the clean combination of flesh and skin with or without accompanying bone, derived from the parts or whole carcasses of chicken or a combination thereof, exclusive of feathers, heads, feet and entrails.
- **Lamb Meal** – the rendered product from lamb tissues, exclusive of blood, hair, hoof, horn, hide trimmings, manure, stomach and rumen contents except in such amounts as may occur unavoidably in good processing practices.
- **Turkey Meal** – the ground clean combination of flesh and skin with or without accompanying bone, derived from the parts or whole carcasses of turkey or a combination thereof, exclusive of feathers, heads, feet and entrails.
- **Meat By-Products** – the non-rendered, clean parts, other than meat, derived from slaughtered mammals. It includes, but is not limited to, lungs, spleen, kidneys, brain, livers, blood, bone, partially defatted low-temperature fatty tissue and stomachs and

intestines freed of their contents. It does not include hair, horns, teeth and hooves.

- **Poultry By-Product Meal** – consists of the ground, rendered, clean parts of the carcass of slaughtered poultry, such as necks, feet, undeveloped eggs, intestines, exclusive of feathers, except in such amounts as might occur unavoidably in good processing practices.

Let's take a closer look at these various proteins:

Named Meat and Fish Proteins

Real named proteins, such as beef, salmon, and chicken, are the least-processed of all the proteins and the ones that we recommend as the first ingredient in your dog's food. Here are some common named proteins (in no particular order):

- Chicken
- Beef
- Salmon
- Lamb
- Whitefish
- Duck
- Herring
- Venison
- Bison
- Turkey
- Pork
- Anchovy
- Sardine
- Pheasant
- Walleye
- Trout
- Kangaroo
- Rabbit
- Goat
- Haddock
- Whiting

Meal

Meal is product that has been ground up and had its water removed. The result is a highly concentrated and processed source of protein. I liken meal to the condensed food that astronauts used to eat on space flights—a temporary solution to their nutrition problem when they had no access to whole foods. For dog foods, meal can be used to increase the amount and percentage of protein in a food. In my view, that is acceptable, especially if meal is not the first ingredient.

By-Products

By-products are essentially the scraps that are left on the animal carcass after all of the meat is stripped away. This is the lowest quality protein choice available, because you don't know what you are actually feeding your dog. Further, the by-product can be relatively indigestible, so the protein that your dog really needs simply passes through their digestive system and ends up as waste. Avoid foods with by-products.

Unnamed Proteins

Unnamed proteins, like "meat," "animal," "poultry," and "fish" are often used as protein or meal sources. Does your dog food contain any of these? If so, switch. These designations are so vague you can have no idea what the ingredient actually is. Even worse—unnamed protein by-product, for example animal by-product. Avoid foods that can't even tell you what is in the recipe!

Non-Meat Sources of Protein

Some foods use non-meat sources of protein such as corn or wheat. These grains are generally difficult for dogs to digest. Brands that use corn, corn meal, wheat, and wheat gluten as main protein sources can technically meet industry standards for protein content, but much of the protein passes right through the dog's system unused. Be wary of foods that contain copious amounts of grains in lieu of meat.

- Steve Pelletier

 *YOU*

Counting Calories

Counting calories is an effective and easy-to-understand tool for weight loss—simply take in fewer calories than you burn. But counting calories can also be tedious and easily abandoned. It's helpful, however, to have a general understanding of how many calories your body needs, and how many you're consuming. This chart shows how many calories an average adult of moderate activity needs to lose weight. [xvii]

	Age (years)	Daily Calories
Females	19-30	< 2000
	31-50	< 1800
	51+	< 1600
Males	19-30	< 2400
	31-50	< 2200
	51+	< 2000

*According to the USDA

You may need more calories if you have an active lifestyle, and less if you are sedentary.

Sedentary- You spend most of your day sitting or standing. You may have an office job or work at the computer all day. You might even call yourself a couch potato!

Moderate Activity- Your job is not physically strenuous, but your day includes light activities, moderate walking, and occasional heavier work. You might participate in a weekly workout class or sport.

Active Lifestyle- You aren't happy unless you engage in physical activity every day. You may have a job involving walking, lifting or both. After work you go to the gym, take a run, or join the team for a game. Weekends are for hiking, swimming, or skiing.

YOUR DOG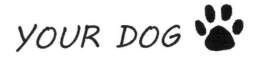

Counting Calories

Consult your veterinarian to determine your dog's specific calorie requirements. This may be affected by your dog's:

- Breed
- Lifestyle
- Age
- Genetics
- Medical conditions
- Activity level

General Calorie Needs for Average Activity Level Dogs[xviii]

Size	Daily Calories
10 pounds	300
20 pounds	500
50 pounds	1200

Your dog may need more calories if your dog has an active lifestyle, and less if your dog is sedentary.

Sedentary– The canine equivalent of a couch potato. Your dog spends most of the day sleeping. Your dog is content with a walk from the living room to the kitchen, and is probably the very best snugglebug ever!

Moderate Activity–Your dog is always up for a walk…but would just as much enjoy a ride in the car. Your dog spends hours playing with you in the yard, and then crashes for a nice nap. Perfect.

Active Lifestyle– The canine athlete. Your dog never seems to stop. Your dog zips around the house in high gear, plays enthusiastically with stuffies, and is not only up for a walk…how about a run?

 *YOU*

Dieting Tips

- Weigh or measure your food so you won't over-estimate serving sizes.

- Learn how to read and understand food labels.

- Sit at the dining table when you eat. Avoid eating in front of the television.

- Have healthy snacks handy in portion-controlled packages.

- Keep fruits and veggies readily visible in the refrigerator.

- Keep a food journal and record what you eat, when you eat, and even your emotions before eating. Be honest. Food you don't record still counts!

- Eat a healthy breakfast every morning to get your day off to a good start.

- Decide if you're really hungry before grabbing a snack. Wait ten minutes to see if your craving disappears.

YOUR DOG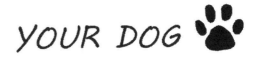

Dieting Tips

- Always measure your dog's food instead of pouring in "one scoop."

- Resist offering your dog table scraps.

- Substitute dog-appropriate fruits and veggies for more fattening treats.

- Keep healthy treats such as baby carrots handy in the refrigerator so they'll be just as easy to grab as a dog biscuit.

- If your dog seems hungry, try mixing a spoon of canned pumpkin (pure pumpkin, not prepared pie filling) with dinner. It's good for digestion and will help your dog feel full.

- When your dog begs for food, go outside, throw a ball, or play tug games for distraction.

 *YOU*

Healthy Snacks

Apples
Grapes
Melon
Carrot and celery sticks
Broccoli spears
Unsalted sunflower seeds
Unsalted almonds
Cherry or grape tomatoes
Strawberries
Raspberries
Low-fat yogurt or Greek yogurt
Unsweetened canned fruit
Angel food cake
Graham cracker
Pita with hummus
Turkey breast
Low-fat, high fiber cereal
Frozen all-fruit popsicles
Whole grain crackers
Fat-free popcorn

YOUR DOG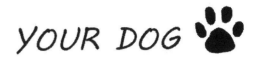

Healthy Snacks

Carrots
Apples (no seeds)
Banana
Rice cake
Watermelon
Blueberries
Green beans (fresh or frozen)
Pumpkin
Sweet potato
Dried sweet potato chips
Dried kale chips
Lean chicken
Healthy low-calorie dog treats

DO **NOT** feed your dog:

Chocolate	Macadamia nuts	Corn cobs
Onions	Coffee/caffeine	Garlic
Grapes	Avocado	Raisins
Fruit pits and apple seeds		Dough/yeast
Anything with xylitol (sweetener)		Alcohol

JUST FOR WOMEN
You and Your Heart

Did you know that excess weight puts you at a greater risk for heart attack, and that more women die from heart disease than any other condition?[xix] Many women, however, don't recognize or report the symptoms. The American Heart Association[xx] explains that this is because women's symptoms often feel different than men's. Women don't always experience crushing chest pain, for example. For women, heart attack symptoms may include:

- Extreme shortness of breath
- Pressure or squeezing in lower chest or upper abdomen
- Pain in the back, one or both arms, neck or jaw
- Dizziness, lightheadedness or fainting
- Nausea
- Extreme fatigue

What You Can Do to Help your Heart:

- Schedule a checkup with your doctor to evaluate your risks
- Improve your diet
- Maintain a healthy weight
- Increase daily exercise
- If you smoke, quit

Exercise

 *YOU*

How Much Exercise?

The American Heart Association recommends all healthy adults (ages 18 to 64) should get at least 2 hours and 30 minutes of moderate-intensity aerobic physical activity every week, or 1 hour and 15 minutes of vigorous-intensity aerobic physical activity every week[xxi]. In addition, they recommend two or more days each week of muscle strengthening activities that work all major muscle groups (legs, hips, back, abdomen, chest, shoulders, and arms). This will help you lose weight, reduce abdominal fat, and preserves muscle during weight loss.

Approximate number of calories burned[xxii]:
(Calculated per one hour of activity, for a 150 lb person.)

Bicycling--240

Walking 3mph--320

Walking 4.5mph--440

Running 5.5mph--660

Running 10mph--1280

Swimming 25 yards/minute--275

Jumping rope--750

*Before starting any exercise program, consult with your doctor to make sure you are fit for exercising.

YOUR DOG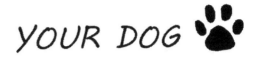

How Much Exercise?

Steve Pelletier is a fitness and exercise enthusiast who often works out with his yellow lab, Jack. But does your dog need as much exercise as Jack? How can you tell? Here's Steve with some answers.

We all know we should encourage our pets to exercise…but how can we tell what is the right amount and what is too much?

Currently, we have two senior dogs, Jack and Maggie, who enjoy keeping active with us. We've always had dogs with certain challenges, but that hasn't stopped us from getting them exercise. One senior lab with orthopedic issues enjoyed swimming. Our shepherd-mix ran with us even though he was blind. And Maggie, our latest addition, was thin–too thin actually–when we adopted her. She had spent her life in a cage as a breeder mom. She had no muscle mass at all and we had to slowly build up her strength and endurance through short walks, then longer walks, until she can now run a few miles a few times a week.

Jack is another story! He was obese when we got him and needed exercise not only to lose the weight, but also to drain his surplus energy.

Jack's Story

In the summer of 2011, our family was ready to adopt a new dog after having lost our beloved Tino. We saw a picture of a Yellow Lab named Suka, who was residing at a no-kill shelter in Southern California. In the picture he was skinny, but had a classic lab look. We arranged to have him visit our home to see if it would be a good fit.

Imagine our surprise when he jumped out of the car onto our front yard--and was one of the fattest labs we had seen! A real doughboy, mostly out of control, panting like crazy. In a nutshell, he was a train wreck.

We came to find out that Suka had been in a shelter for more than a year. He was placed a few times but was returned due to bad behaviors. Suka was on the anti-depressant medication Prozac for his behavioral issues and Rimadyl for joint pain. We decided to adopt him, as we felt that he had spent enough time looking for a forever home. The first thing we did was change his name to Jack which, for us, fit him better.

We really weren't sure how our experience with Jack was going to evolve, but we knew two things: 1) Jack was not going to weigh 105 pounds and 2) Jack was not going to remain on Prozac. To my mind, the best way to approach both of these issues was with proper exercise and diet. We took Jack to our veterinarian and learned that Jack's ideal weight was about 85 pounds, and that his 20 pound weight loss target should be met gradually over the course of two to four months.

To prepare for Jack's weight loss transformation, I combed research articles on canine metabolism and weight loss and created a set of formulas, based partly on the Waltham Center research[1] to estimate how much we should feed Jack based on his activity levels. We began Jack's exercise routine gradually, starting with short walks, then progressing to longer walks, walks with a weighted pack, and then finally running. As we do with our own workout routine, we alternated "easy" and "hard" days each week so that Jack could build strength and recover properly.

By the end of 11 weeks, Jack had reached his goal and weighed 85 pounds. We were able to taper him off Prozac during this period as well, and his mood and behavior improved after he was off this medication.

Jack looked great and became truly fit. He built up his stamina so that a five mile run was easy for him. Now he runs three to four times a week for 35-40 minutes and walks for 20-30 minutes at least twice a day.

Once his weight was more appropriate for his frame, he was able to stop taking the Rimadyl as he no longer exhibited any indications of joint pain.

There's no one-size answer for how much exercise your dog needs, or even what type of exercise they need. The only constant is that they all need some form of exercise. Even your little guys need to move their muscles!

Can there be Too Much Exercise?

Yes, there absolutely is such a thing as too much exercise for your pet, just as there is for people. You see those people at the gym, obsessed with their body fat, causing more damage than good by the extreme nature of their methods. Dogs won't do that to themselves, but we can push them too far if we aren't watchful of the signs that they don't feel up to that level of activity. Maybe one of their limbs is sore or they are just tired. Each pet has different exercise needs. As a responsible pet parent, you need to read your pet's behavior and response to the exercise you provide and react according to your dog's needs. Some signals that you need to cut back or give your dog a break:

- Excessive panting during or after the exertion
- Lagging behind on a run/walk when your dog is normally in front
- Any lameness or limping
- Extreme thirst
- Appearing to be overtired after the exercise, sleeping or laying down more than normal
- Reluctance to go out for the walk, run or to play
- Missing cues or commands your dog knows well

When needed, take walks instead of runs, or take more frequent but shorter walks rather than one long walk. Limit the

Jack is a fit dog!

number of fetches in the front yard. Swimming is a good alternative if your dog has joint problems. If, for some reason, you need to cut back on activity for more than a few days, be sure to adjust your dog's feedings or your dog will start to put on weight. And remember, as your dog ages, less exercise is needed. Adjust your dog's feeding to reflect changes in activity level so that senior dogs don't slowly add weight. Any excess baggage can really place a burden on a senior's joints and tendons. Common sense and

moderation should be your goals. If they are, you will be able to exercise together for your pet's entire life…and by doing so, you will increase your dog's longevity and be able to spend more time together. And isn't that the best reward?

- Steve Pelletier

Your furry fitness buddy suggests using hand weights in your workout.

 *YOU*

How to Get Started with Exercise

Eighty percent of Americans don't make exercise a regular habit, and, according to an American Heart Association survey, 14 percent say they don't like to exercise.[xxiii] You may not necessarily find exercise fun, but these tips can help make the experience a bit easier.

- Choose an activity that fits your lifestyle. You're more likely to stick with it.
- **Start your day with exercise. That way you won't get too tired or busy to fit it in later.**
- Get your friends and family involved with you.
- **Walk and talk. I often chat on my cell phone while walking the dog.**
- Walk some place you find pleasurable, like a park or shore.
- **Wear a pedometer and aim for increasing the number of steps you take each day.**
- Set goals. My husband set a goal to run a 5K—and succeeded!
- **Join a sports team, exercise group, or fitness club.**
- Take up a new active hobby like ice skating or Pilates.
- **Dance. One of my friends found interpretive dancing to praise music just right for her body and soul.**
- Find ways to sneak in extra activity, such as taking the stairs or parking farther away from the door at the grocery store.
- **Stand up and exercise during the TV commercials.**
- Remember, almost anything is more fun when you do it with your dog!

YOUR DOG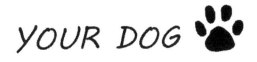

How to Get Started with Exercise

- Start with short walks around the block or in the park.
- **Play with your dog. Use balls and squeaky toys to catch your dog's attention.**
- Make an obstacle course for your dog in your back yard. Try obstacles to jump over and climb under.
- **Use interactive toys such as puzzle balls for a portion of your dog's daily meals. Your dog will burn calories while working for the food.**
- Participate in dog walks for various causes, such as *Bark for Life,* which benefits cancer research.
- **If your dog plays well with others, arrange doggie play dates. They're great for burning calories.**
- Consider agility or other dog sports that your dog might enjoy. (See the list on page 73)
- **Be careful not to overwork your dog. Understand your dog's capabilities, and consider your dog's health, age, and activity level.**
- Consider conditions—adjust your outdoor workouts when the weather is too hot or too cold.
- **Don't force your dog to do something your dog is not enjoying. Switch to a different activity.**
- Remember to always have water available. Keep Fido hydrated!

Doggone Excuses

If there was a way to avoid exercise, I found it.

Aerobics? Bad knees.

Personal trainer? Too expensive.

Treadmill? No room.

"There's one exercise I bet you can't dismiss," my husband challenged. "Walking. It's free, easy, and you don't need any special equipment."

But I had an excuse.

I used to take walks. Lacing up my sneakers and hitching a leash to my spunky little spaniel's collar, we'd hit the pavement together. Kelly's tail waved like a banner, her nose lifted high taking in the mossy green scent of spring or the crisp autumn air. Walking with my dog, exercise was actually enjoyable.

Kelly never lets cooler weather deter her from taking a walk.

Until one day when Kelly and I were strolling through a park adjoining my neighborhood. She wandered at the end of her leash along a bank that sloped down toward a river. Watching her curious exploration, I didn't notice anyone else around us until an alarming, hulking shape appeared--a dog big enough to eclipse the sun, ears flat, teeth bared.

I'm not usually afraid of dogs. But when I saw that huge, vicious-looking creature barreling straight toward us, I almost jumped in the river.

In the large, grassy openness there wasn't even a scrawny sapling to shield us. My grip tightened on Kelly's leash, my mind filled with fear that my pampered pooch would soon serve as an appetizer for the lunging behemoth. The dog bore down. I froze in terror. But Kelly yanked ahead, her fur standing on end all the way from her neck to the tip of her long, feathery tail. She wasn't afraid at all. She thought she could take that bad boy.

Then, in the distance, a young man wearing a hoodie sweatshirt whistled. The dog hesitated, turned and bolted back to its owner.

I was safely home in my easy chair before my breathing returned to normal. If dangerous dogs roamed the park, they could be anywhere. Loose dogs in the alleys, behind the railroad tracks. Even on my own street I'd noticed a burly dog dragging a broken length of chain. What about those stories of mistreated, mishandled fighting dogs? I lifted Kelly protectively onto my lap. "No more walks for us, girl." With that, I'd found an excuse to avoid exercise again.

Over the next few weeks I attempted a workout DVD, but plopped back down on the couch before working up a sweat. Those lithe ladies didn't inspire me to get moving. Before long I glanced down at my jeans' waistband straining at the seams. While Kelly could run around in the back yard, that didn't solve my fitness needs. Maybe walking was the best exercise, but I was too afraid to face the prospect of another loose dog.

One Saturday as I sat working at my desk, Kelly lounged with her head propped up on the sofa arm, staring wistfully out the window. Was she missing the walks, the change of scenery, the enticing scents? I got up and joined her at the window. Children scampered off a school bus. A woman with a stroller passed by. The scene didn't look as threatening as I imagined.

Day after day Kelly continued to stare, heaving heavy sighs, legs sprawled over the edge of the couch. I felt as lethargic as she looked. Although I didn't relish exercise, my body began to feel the effects of immobility. Heavy. Tired. Sluggish. Something in Kelly's deep, brown eyes urged me to get outside, for myself as much as for her. I glanced at the door. Maybe we'd try a short walk again.

Kelly jumped like a toy on a spring as I snapped on her leash. I looked up and down the street twice before venturing out the door. "Just one spin around the block," I said as Kelly marched beside me.

"C'mon Mom, let's take a walk!"

Peering between houses and behind parked cars, I listened for threatening snarls. White knuckles clenched the leash. *This is no way to walk,* I thought, ready to turn back. Kelly, however, trotted eagerly ahead, pulling me along behind her, unconcerned about what might lie around the corner. She wasn't letting that close call in the park prevent her from enjoying her walk. In fact, when we'd encountered that huge dog she'd faced it bravely, ready to use whatever strength she had to run him off. Didn't I have at least as much might and courage as my fearless spaniel? I loosened my grip and moved ahead. Staying alert to my surroundings, I could spot a potential situation before a problem arose. If need be, I could change directions or cross the street. I even could grab my cell phone if I really needed help.

Then, from behind, I heard the scratching of paws on the pavement. A raspy snort; a menacing warning. Every muscle in my body tensed, my fear realized. A loose dog—coming right at us.

I spun around. The terrifying canine stood about ankle high. Long, caramel fur fell from a red bow on the top of its head, around its pushed-in nose and dainty ears. A little rhinestone studded collar surrounded its neck. Four tiny paws scampered at our feet. "Yip!" it barked.

Fear quickly evaporated as I laughed out loud. Kelly casually sniffed the miniature dog. The pup gave one last yip and left, and we continued on our way.

When we got home I hung the leash in the hall, and Kelly stared up at me with her soft, wide eyes. "We'll go out again tomorrow," I promised, patting her head. Maybe I was still wary of loose dogs, but that wouldn't stop me from taking our walk. With exercise, just like in life, hurdles may appear larger than they truly are. And, although I may be expecting a Great Dane size obstacle, often I find it's only the size of a Pomeranian.

Walking With Your Dog

"Wanna go for a walk?"

Those are magic words for most dogs! My dogs jump, try to grab their leashes off the hook, and spring for the door. But there are times the walk itself becomes a bit routine. Here are some ways to get more out of your walks together.

Kelly tries to show Brooks the right way to go.

1. Take a different route--If your walk is getting boring, try turning left instead of right. If you always go to the same park, try one across town. Meet a friend and walk in her neighborhood. Or even doing your same route backwards might give you a new outlook and put a spring in your step.

2. Carry weights--Walking may give many dogs a hearty workout, but isn't always strenuous enough for us. For an extra calorie burn, carry hand weights when you walk.

3. Try intervals--You and your dog may not be up for a flat-out run

50

(yet), so try running for a short sprint, maybe one block or one minute, then walk for 5 minutes, then sprint again. If you and your dog are up for the challenge, you may find it breaks the boredom of the regular old walk and gets you both nice and fit.

4. Combine fitness with leisure--Walk briskly on the first half of your walk, and then take a more leisurely stroll on the way back.

5. Make it fun--Whatever you do, be sure to make it enjoyable for both of you!

Good friends walk together.

Running with Your Dog

Snoopy the Bearded Collie is not only good looking, and a therapy dog, but also a fit dog! His Mom Annette Vivian enjoys keeping fit right along with him. One of their favorite activities is running.

Two dogs are double the fun on Annette's run.

I started running with my dog Snoopy about two years ago. Shortly afterwards, we invited our neighbor's dog, Cosmo, to join us. Over time I've learned how to make running with dogs easier, safer and more fun.

First, consult both your doctor and your veterinarian to ensure you and your dog are fit enough to run. Snoopy was less than a year old when we started running, so my vet advised starting off by running half a mile each day and increasing by another half mile every two weeks. My vet said, "Eventually Snoopy will be able to outrun you. After all, he's a herding dog, you know!" My vet was right! So just bear in mind your breed of dog and if they are capable of, or interested in, running longer distances.

The right stuff

Once you get the okay for both you and your dog to run, make sure you have the proper gear. It's totally possible to run in old tennis shoes, regular shorts and a t-shirt. To prevent injury and feel comfortable, however, I recommend getting good running shoes, proper running socks and running clothes (including underwear) that will keep you cooler in the heat and warmer in the cold. I usually get my gear at outlet stores; you can find some great deals. It's worth the money to invest in the proper gear.

Now on to the dog's running gear. Sure, you can just attach their lead to their collar and off you go. I've discovered, however, that a harness works best for Snoopy. I think it's more comfortable and safer for him. He still wears a collar with ID tags. I also have him wear a GPS tag system on his collar so I could track him using my cell phone if we got separated.

I like to use a lead that has padded grips so it doesn't chafe my skin if the dog pulls or suddenly stops. I also like to clip the lead onto my running belt. This is really useful when I'm cleaning up after my dog, so I can easily use both hands and not have to drop the lead. I also attach a poo bag holder to the lead, and take my cell phone in case of emergencies.

Training your dog to run

So, now that we have all the equipment, we're ready to go! Running with a dog isn't as easy as running on your own. You have to keep stopping, you have to train your dog to run with

Always use proper gear.

you, and you have to remain vigilant that you don't fall over your dog or run into any danger. However, for me it does mean that I go out every day. Snoopy *loves* to go running! Every morning he encourages me to get moving and even starts barking if I take too long. We go out in all weather; windy, chilly, rainy. We live in California so I can't pretend it's *that* bad, but without his encouragement I'd probably skip those less desirable days!

When running, I use a number of commands that Snoopy has learned over time, such as "Wait," "This way,"(when we're changing direction,) and "Okay," (if we've had to run on the road and we're going to return to the sidewalk).

When Snoopy was a puppy, running would sometimes get him overexcited. When this happened I would just stop and ask him to sit until he relaxed, and then we could carry on. As he's grown, Snoopy displays more self-control and responds well to my leash corrections. This makes running together a pleasure.

Most importantly, you should be mindful of injuries. If Snoopy or I become injured, we switch to walking until we're fit enough to run again. Taking it easy and knowing your limits are good ways to help prevent injuries. You may want to avoid too many hills, as they can add additional stress to joints and muscles.

If you start to get a few injuries, look at the condition of your running shoes. A general rule of thumb is to get new running shoes every 500 miles, although this is only a guide. You may be reluctant to spend the money on new shoes, but trust me, I learned the hard way that shoes are way cheaper than medical bills!

Double Trouble

If you have more than one dog, or want to give a friend's dog some exercise, you may want to run with two dogs! This takes a little more practice.

First, I worked on walking with Snoopy and Cosmo together. I use harnesses for both dogs, and then I attach both harnesses to a split lead which I attach to the main lead. All the clips have spinning connections to help avoid tangles. When we first started to go out together, Snoopy got overexcited and wanted to play with Cosmo rather than walk. So I had to be patient and eventually they worked it out. They also worked out how to get untangled, and how to wait for each other if one of them is busy.

The important things to remember are to plan, train, stay safe, be consistent and don't give up. Running is a great way to spend quality time with your dog and to get fit at the same time. Sometimes it's difficult to motivate yourself to get out the door and go--when I first started running about four years ago, I hated it. Then I discovered running with Snoopy and Cosmo. Now I'm nearly as addicted as the dogs!

- Annette Vivian

Snoopy waits patiently for his next run.

 **YOU**

A Running Program

If you are interested in running, you may enjoy training for races, such as a 5K, 10K, half marathon or even a marathon. You can find training groups and running programs to help you prepare. The Couch to 5K ® Running Plan by Cool Running[xxiv] is one such program, designed to get just about anyone from the couch to running 5 kilometers (3.1 miles) in 30 minutes in just nine weeks.

Because so many people either have no idea how to start running, or try to start off too fast, they often become frustrated and quit. Couch to 5K ® training plan helps ease you into running longer distances.

The program alternates walking and running, gradually decreasing the amount of time you walk, and increasing the amount of time you run. You can follow the program outside or on a treadmill. Even if you aren't planning on running a race, this program will help get you fit.

Runners start off on a 5K.

YOUR DOG

A Running Program

Pooch to 5K, developed by Australian veterinarian Audrey Harvey, is a program designed to get your dog running 5 kilometers in just 12 weeks. Harvey was inspired to create the program as a result of her passion for preventative health care and obesity management in dogs. She developed the program along with her husband Francis Harvey, who has a background in dog training and obedience, and is a runner and accredited athletics coach.

"Veterinarians are becoming more and more concerned about the increase in joint pain, heart disease and other obesity related illnesses in dogs. Dogs can't lift weights, or use the gym. If you're going to increase their fat burning, you need to increase the intensity of their exercise," says Harvey. The Pooch to 5k program will help you get your dog from doing nothing much, to comfortably running 5km. Because you'll be running with your dog, you'll also get a great workout!

Audrey and friends enjoy a scenic run.

Hiking with your Dog

Sarah Burdo is a veterinary technician and a Vermonter who fully enjoys the state's Green Mountains, hiking with her Rottweiler Charlie and her Chihuahua Homie, proving that hiking is great for any breed and size!

Sarah, Charlie and Homie atop Snake Mountain.

I never really hiked until I got my boy Charlie. My best friend invited me on a hike up Vermont's Mount Mansfield, so I grabbed the leash and off we went! Charlie was still a puppy, and he did great. After that, I was addicted. Now, I would never think to go on a hike without at least one dog. The more the merrier!

58

Sarah and 2-legged and 4-legged friends enjoy the view.

Know your Dog

You never want to attempt a hike that is too strenuous for your dog. I take a lot of hikes on various terrains, and would never ask my dog to tackle one that was too difficult. I know my dogs so well that I can tell if they can't handle something and we need to turn around. It's all about being able to read your dog's signs and to understand what your dog needs. Charlie and Homie so far have been able to handle every hike I've taken them on.

5 Things You Should Know Before Leaving on a Hike

1. Check the weather before you leave for a hike. Be very mindful of excessive heat or cold. Either can cause serious medical emergencies with your hiking buddy.
2. Make sure you are prepared for emergencies.
3. Start out doing short hikes and work your way up to the bigger ones.
4. Watch out for porcupines!
5. Be mindful of other hikers- not everybody wants a dog slobbering all over them...weirdos!

Looking for something good inside the backpack.

5 Most Important Items to Bring on a Hike
1. Water
2. Leash
3. Poo bags
4. Food/snack
5. Vet wrap (you never know when someone's going to cut their pad)

The items may vary depending on the season, but these would be my staples. I'm a vet tech, so I also tend to bring a backpack of different medical supplies...just in case.

-   Sarah Burdo

Footprints in the Vermont snow.

Dogs of all breeds and sizes enjoy hiking.

Backpacking with your Dog

Jessica Rhae leads an active life with her two adventurous dachshunds, Chester and Gretel. As President of the Adventureweiner Club of Seattle, her goal is to raise awareness of the importance of keeping pets active, and at a healthy weight.

Make sure your dog is included in your camping gear!

Hiking and backpacking with my dogs are soul-nourishing activities for me. It gives me time to step away from the busyness of life and get more in-tune with Chester and Gretel and strengthen our bond. The challenges also make me mentally and physically stronger.

Here are some general points to keep in mind when preparing you and your dog to go backpacking:

- Make sure you and your dog are up to the physical challenge by walking and completing several shorter day hikes leading up to the trip.

- Before you go, make sure dogs are allowed on the trail. Follow good hiking etiquette with your dog.
- Certain locations require passes to park at the trailhead or overnight camping permits. Make sure you have the proper permits before you go.
- You should always leave your itinerary with someone and check in with them when you get back. That way they can alert the proper authorities if you don't return on time. It's also a good idea to leave your itinerary in the glove box of your car or under the seat.
- Avoid cotton clothing, including socks, because when cotton gets wet it will no longer keep you warm. Wearing a cotton shirt to hike in the heat of a summer day is okay, but always bring along wicking, quick drying clothing for other times.
- Both you and your dog will be burning a lot of energy and will require more food and water than you consume regularly. Plan on packing extra snacks and drinks.
- Look up the address and phone number of an emergency vet close to where you will be hiking in the unfortunate event something happens to your dog.
- Pack a couple of no-sodium bouillon cubes to add to your dog's water in case your dog won't drink. Sometimes dogs are too distracted or uncomfortable drinking in a strange place and it is very important they stay hydrated.
- In addition to regular camp gear, don't forget to pack baby wipes, duct tape, trash bags, extra socks, rain gear, dog bedding, and poo bags.
- Remember safety essentials such as a first aid kit, topographic map (on waterproof paper and in a large plastic bag), compass, lighter and waterproof matches, sunscreen, headlamp with extra batteries, small pocket knife and emergency whistle.

-    Jessica Rhae

Biking with your Dog

Kate Richards promotes an active lifestyle for people who love dogs. She lives in Australia, and loves to go bike riding, or cycling, along with her dog Scooter.

Scooter and Kate

Biking with your dog is an excellent way to keep fit and exercise your dog, particularly if your dog has tons of energy. Before you grab the leash and head out the gate, there are a few questions you should ask yourself:

How healthy is my dog?

Biking with a dog can be an intense workout for the animal. Is your dog fit enough to jog over an extended period? Have your dog examined by your veterinarian to be sure. I suggest short bike rides initially. This will allow you and your dog to get used to the exercise. Your dog may wish to gallop, but a slow trot is best and will reduce the risk of your dog overheating.

How emotionally mature is my dog?

Can your dog understand basic commands? It's important for you to have good control over your dog while he is running beside you. For most dogs this happens around one year old. Each dog is different though – I had to wait until my dog reached three! It's essential that your dog will keep moving when you're riding a bike with them. Sudden stops can cause all sorts of problems!

Have I got the right equipment?

A harness and a strong, solid lead are your minimum requirements (after the dog and bike of course!). A neck collar will cause your dog discomfort and possibly injury. A harness around the dog's body will help transfer the weight better. The lead should be the non-extending variety and should be attached to the bike at a secure point – preferably around your bike's center of gravity (I find just under the seat works best for me). If you're not keen to tie your dog off to the bike, you can buy a specialized attachment that will detach in an emergency.

To attach the leash onto the bike, I use a tether such as what is used to attach a dog harness to your car's seatbelt. I take my bike's seat off and slip the belt part of the tether onto my seat post and make it sit above my rear reflector. You need to keep this part high on the seat post, because if the attachment slips down, the leash can become entangled with the back tire. My leg and body remain in front of the leash once attached. I find that my leg acts as a brace if my dog pulls and keeps my dog enough distance away from my bike.

Scooter keeps a nice pace with the bike.

Are conditions safe?

Gears? Check! Tires? Check! Brakes? Check! Safety helmet? Check! It also helps if you're a confident cyclist. Ensure that you and your bike are ready for the road trip. Keep your dog on the side that is away from traffic – if your dog pulls, it should take you away from the road, not into it. Also make sure you keep your dog away from the front of your bike. Do not attempt to ride with the dog's leash in your hand – a dog can easily float in front of your wheel or pull your handlebars in the wrong direction – it's an accident waiting to happen.

And finally, practice in a safe place before attempting to ride anywhere near traffic. I do a quick suburban hop during the early morning hours to some fields nearby, where my dog can run freely beside me. This way he gets the opportunity to put his head down for a sniff or two. It also gives us both a chance to set our own pace while out exercising together.

Out on the open trail, your dog can run free.

Bike where there is the least amount of traffic or choose a time when it's not peak hours. Another thing I've learned is that it's important that people notice that you're traveling with a dog attached. Make sure your dog is wearing a bright colored lead or harness to help attract attention.

Remember these important steps and you'll have fun:
1. Use a harness and safe equipment.
2. Keep your dog mainly trotting beside you for the best workout and to prevent overheating.
3. Use simple commands to let your dog know you are turning or slowing down.

4. Try going off-road if you can – it will give you a better workout and be softer on your dog's paws.
5. Carry a saddlebag with treats to help focus your dog's attention back onto you.

- Kate Richards

Shadow play on a morning cycle run.

Climbing Stairs with Your Dog

Stair exercises are an excellent workout for both you and your dog. Rosalyn and Sugar climb stairs regularly, and Rosalyn even participates in annual climb competitions.

Good job, Sugar!

When I was recovering from ankle and hip injuries, my doctor recommended stair exercises to help me regain motion control. These exercises provided an excellent workout for my legs, shoulders, hips, and lower back. Stair climbing is good for dogs as well. It is more intense than running, as each step requires lifting the dog's entire body weight through the height of the stair. Going down the stairs involves negative contraction, which intensifies the workout. Stair exercise also helps a dog with coordination and agility.

How to Get Started

1. Make sure your dog knows basic commands such as "heel," "sit" and "stay."
2. Start on a short flights of steps.
3. At the bottom of the steps, ask your dog to sit or stand at your side. Then go up the stairs with the command "heel."
4. If your dog is skilled at heeling off leash, go ahead and remove the leash. If not, we recommend using a short leash. A 24" leash will allow better control and help your dog stay by your side during your stair exercise.
5. Once you reach the top step, turn and ask your dog to sit or stand at your side again. Give the "heel" command and go back down the stairs.

It takes a lot of patience and practice to do stair exercises with your dog. When you get it right and go up and down side by side, the feeling of being in sync is an awesome achievement.

- Rosalyn Acero

Climbing stairs in sync.

69

Snowshoeing with your Dog

Jessica, Chester and Gretel keep fitness going all year round. More snow means more fun!

Gretel and Chester stay warm in the snow.

Snowshoeing is almost as easy as hiking. It takes a little more effort, but just think of it as hiking a steeper version of a trail. If you can walk, you can snowshoe.

Snowshoeing is a fun and easily-accessible activity which has become one of the fastest-growing winter sports. In the last decade, the number of people who identify themselves as snowshoers has grown by 60% . Snowshoes are designed to keep you floating on top of the snow. Unfortunately they don't make snowshoes for dogs. But your dog can still enjoy joining you on the trails.

If the snow is hard and crusty on top, your small, light dog isn't likely to sink into the snow very far. If the snow is soft, however, your dog may find it difficult to walk, especially if you have a short dog.

One solution is to snowshoe where there is compacted snow, such as groomed cross country ski trails (don't walk in the skiers' tracks – stay off to the side) and popular hiking trails where people have already beaten a path.

As a last resort, you can make your own trail and your dog can walk behind you. It works best if you have two people on snowshoes, because one can stomp on the snow that the other's footsteps didn't compact.

To make sure you have an enjoyable trip, you will also need the right gear. You and your dog will need more layers of clothing to stay comfortable out in the cold. We recommend an extra-thick jacket for your dog and something to protect their feet. You can use booties if your dog will wear them, or Musher's Secret balm is a good option for your dog's paws.

You may think of snowshoes as huge tennis rackets you strap to your feet. Those went away about 15 or 20 years ago! Today's snowshoes are shorter, narrower, lighter, and generally have a raised toe, more like skis.

Modern snowshoes.

If you're not accustomed to snowshoeing, start with short walks on flat ground. Gradually increase the distance, and add some hilly terrain. After that, you can progress to longer treks. Keep in mind that when you move to deeper snow, you may have to scale back--if you were hiking four miles on packed snow, aim for two or three miles in deep snow.

Snowshoeing is so much fun that you almost forget you are exercising!

- Jessica Rhae

What's cuter than two little dogs in the snow, here in the Cascade Mountains?

YOUR DOG

Sports for Dogs

Agility—obstacle course through tunnels, weave poles and hurdles
Flyball—relay race with a tennis ball and hurdles
Treibball—sport involving large exercise balls and a soccer goal
Dock diving—water sport where dogs dive and compete for distance
Rally-O—obedience competition with handler encouragement
Retrieving—fetching and delivering a ball or object
Disc dog—chasing and jumping to catch a flying disc
Herding—farm or ranch work with sheep or other livestock
Heelwork—a routine where the dog stays at a heel, may be done to music
Canine Freestyle—obedience, tricks and dance
Nose work—using scent to find concealed objects
Tracking—using scent or clues to follow a track
Lure coursing—chasing a lure across a field
Surfing—riding the waves on a surfboard

Havanese Rocco hangs ten....er, twenty!

 # YOUR DOG

Agility

Diane Silver has trained all types of dogs in agility for both fun and competition, and has competed in agility with her Havanese since 2004.

Cosmo flies over the jump.

Getting Started in Agility

The agility competitors you see on television or at local events make this sport look effortless. Teaching your dog to weave in and out of poles and traverse the moving plank known as a teeter, however, takes time and patience.

The good news is that agility is easy to learn. Whether you have aspirations of competing, or are just looking for a great way to get some exercise, agility is a fun way for you to get fit while strengthening the bond between you and your dog.

How to get started

1. **Check out an agility trial** in your area to learn more about the sport. Chat with local competitors, too. Between runs, agility competitors typically are happy to share information about how they got started and where they train. Search for events in your area hosted by the American Kennel Club, the United States Dog Agility Association and the North American Dog Agility Council.
2. **Learn basic obedience**, such as sit, down, stay and come. In your first few agility classes, you may spend time brushing up on basic obedience before getting on any equipment. Your instructor can advise the best class for your current level of experience.
3. **Locate a training club** in your area and take a class. The AKC and USDAA offer listings on their sites. Taking a class from an experienced instructor will help you learn to run competently and safely. The club contact can help find the right class for you.

Most importantly, have fun! Enjoy the time you spend with your dog and you'll both have fun at agility for years to come!

- Diane Silver

Rocco dashes through the tunnel.

 *YOU*

Swimming

Shadow, Milo and Marley join in the fun.

Spending time in the pool or lake can help you burn calories and tone your arms, legs and core. Water's buoyancy supports your body and allows for a workout that is easy on your bones and joints.

Pool Workouts:
Kick
Swim laps
Tread water
Play tag games
Dive for objects
Do water exercises

YOUR DOG

Swimming

You might call Sugar the Golden Retriever a water hound. She started swimming at 11 weeks old! When Rosalyn Acero lived in Hawaii for a year, she brought Sugar to swim in the ocean several times a week. Although they've left the palm trees and Hawaiian breezes behind, Sugar still loves to swim.

Sugar demonstrates the doggy paddle.

Swimming is an excellent low-impact, total body conditioning activity. For an active senior dog like Sugar, swimming will always be on her to-do list.

We used to take Sugar swimming in a lake when she was young, but her Golden Retriever skin didn't do well with the quality of the lake water. So now, an indoor pool is the only option. In our area, most of the indoor pools that allow dogs are built for canine hydro-therapy. Canine hydrotherapy was developed for rehabilitation and treating dogs' injuries.

Benefits of swimming in warm water and a controlled environment:
- Builds muscles
- Reduces stiffness in the joints
- Lessens stress on joints and muscles
- Improves circulation
- Provides anti-inflammatory relief
- Improves overall well-being

Nowadays, many dogs use canine hydrotherapy as a form of exercise to help maintain a desired fitness level. Our vet told us that a 20-25 minute swim is equivalent to about a 4-5 mile walk.

Dog hydrotherapy pools tend to be smaller than human swimming pools. The water is safely treated and heated to 88-92 degrees, which helps relax muscles. The warm water allows for a decrease in pain, muscle spasms and stiffness.

Retrieving objects in the water keeps Sugar active.

Even though Sugar is a good swimmer, she is required to wear a safety vest in the hydrotherapy pool. The harness on the vest is used to guide her in the pool. A bench at the edge of the pool serves as a resting place.

The doggy paddle (usually the first stroke used to teach young children how to swim) is a simple and easy manner of moving in the water. While in the water, your dog simply lies on his or her chest and moves the front leg and back leg alternately. It is like running on land. You might be surprised that many dogs don't instinctively know how to swim.

5 Dog Swimming Tips

1. Use a life jacket, especially for dogs who are not natural swimmers.
2. Never leave your dog to figure it out on his or her own. In the beginning, join your dog in the water.
3. Lead your dog into the water with encouragement.
4. For some dogs, getting wet for the first time is enough. Don't expect your dog to learn how to swim in the first session. Be patient.
5. Provide a floatable toy with which your dog can play. Make your dog's swim a fun game.

Not all dogs enjoy getting wet or being in the water. Sugar is a typical retriever; she enjoys getting wet and loves to swim.

- Rosalyn Acero

 *YOU*

Treadmill

Michele Cuke is a former national class athlete and is now a personal trainer devoted to helping women get fit.

Great form on the treadmill.

A treadmill is a great piece of exercise equipment for an excellent cardiovascular workout. It offers stable footing, varying intensity, and can be used when the weather does not permit outdoor exercise.

Tips:
1. Get familiar with the treadmill's control panel.
2. Know the safety features.
3. Start slowly.
4. If you're a novice, hold on to the handles at first, but aim to be able to work out without holding on.
5. Based on your fitness level, increase your pace to jogging or running.
6. Make the workout more challenging by changing the speed and/or incline.
7. Make sure you change your routine in some way (intensity or time on treadmill) at least every 3-4 months to encourage improvement.

-   Michele Cuke

YOUR DOG

Treadmill

Krista Wickens is a dedicated athlete and co-inventor of the award-winning DogTread® dog treadmill, K9FITvest™ and the StayBall® Balance Ball.

Choose special treadmills designed for your smaller dog.

Has your vet told you that your dog needed "weight loss management?" Maybe you've been given advice to put your dog on a diet and, especially, to fit in more exercise.

Exercise provides physical and mental stimulation and improves overall health. One of the best conditioning exercises for a dog is the extended trot. The diagonal pairs of legs are moving simultaneously, working both sides of the body evenly. The front paw and back paw on the opposite side are both reaching or extending. Most dogs need to do this type of exercise for 20 minutes continuously to achieve the most benefit.

When you take Rover for a walk, it's difficult to measure 20 minutes of continuous moving when he stops to sniff everything along the way and visit with other dogs and passersby. You need some alternatives to get your dog moving and keep him moving. The answer lies in a concept that has been used more commonly in recent years for rehabilitation of an injury, but is now gaining momentum quickly in the dog behavior and training world, as well as being used to combat the ever-increasing problem of dog obesity: the dog treadmill.

Let's dismantle the idea that treadmilling for dogs means you are lazy and never do anything else with your dog. Remember, it's an alternative. That means you can combine walks outside, playing ball, and weekend hikes with time on the treadmill. Those days you don't have enough time for other activities, the treadmill is always there, and you can get your dog moving on it while you are home with the kids, doing a little work from your home office laptop, or exercising on your own treadmill.

Properly designed dog treadmills that promote a full range of motion are excellent tools to help dogs get consistent exercise with purpose and intensity. Intensity is necessary for caloric burn and endorphin release. Intensity and consistency is often missing from the average walk around the block or evening stroll. It is the reason that dog treadmills have a purpose in dog fitness.

A treadmill that is designed for the way a dog moves helps to develop strength and endurance. It is especially important to choose a size that fits your dog's unique size and stride. Too short or too long and it will interfere with your dog's gait.

Tips:
1. Always introduce your dog to a dog treadmill in a positive and rewarding manner.
2. Your confidence is portrayed to your dog - keep your energy positive.
3. Never tie your dog to a treadmill - you cannot assist your dog fast enough if something should happen.

4. Choose a treadmill made for a dog - not a human. A dog's anatomy was never considered in the human designs. Proper gait, range of motion and compliance can easily be disrupted using a treadmill that is not properly-sized.
5. Mix it up - integrate different speeds and inclines to build and tone different muscles. It will challenge your dog's brain as well.
6. Use a dog treadmill as a supplement to outdoor activities - do not replace outdoor time. Dogs need various types of stimulation.

Professional dog trainers find that starting a treadmill program gives dogs more consistent exercise. Working on a dog treadmill aids in training your dog to walk nicely on a leash without pulling, a problem that quickly disappears from getting accustomed to moving continuously. You'll end up with a well-behaved dog you can take out to dog-friendly venues in your city, as well as a great training partner.

Do your dog a big favor. Start treading. Weigh less. Wag more.

\- Krista Wickens

A large dog sets the pace on a treadmill just his size.

 *YOU*

Balance Ball

A variety of exercises can be performed on the balance ball.

Performing sit ups on the balance ball strengthens your core.

The balance ball can also be called the body ball, stability ball, fitness ball, or exercise ball.

Use a balance ball to make your workout more challenging. Balancing on the ball creates instability, which causes other muscles to be recruited and worked. This helps prepare your body for more challenging strength work and also helps improve function in day-to-day activities.

Every part of the body can be worked by using a balance ball, however it is especially helpful to work what is identified as the core. The core is mostly the abdomen and lower back. Core muscles are used in every exercise and physical activity.

The balance ball is a perfect piece of equipment for intensifying your workout and challenging the muscles involved with balance, coordination, and posture.

Tips:
1. Select the correct size balance ball for your height.
2. Inflate the ball firmly.
3. Brace the ball with pillows or towels to prevent it from rolling.
4. Crunches, squats, leg-raises and push-ups are just some of the exercises you can perform on the balance ball.
5. Even just sitting on the ball helps tone your abdominals!

 -   Michele Cuke

This exercise works your hips and thighs.

 # YOUR DOG

Balance Ball

Fitness trainer Diana Ozimek helps people and dogs get fit and have fun.

Make sure you hold the ball steady.

Working with a balance ball is a fun exercise for your smaller dog. This exercise will help your dog develop muscle strength and balance.

86

Place a balance ball against the wall and keep it still, by placing your knee or hand against the other side. Place your dog carefully on the ball. Keep one hand near your dog to help with balance until your dog feels more secure and gets used to the new surface.

Start by letting your dog stay on the ball as long as your dog feels comfortable. If it's only a few seconds, that is fine. Let your dog get down and praise your dog for a great job! Encourage your dog to gradually increase the time on the ball. Your dog's legs and core will strengthen to allow a longer time balancing on top.

For a more advanced workout:

After mastering the basics, try asking your dog to jump up onto the ball. Be sure you are holding the ball stable so it doesn't move when your dog lands.

Looks like a long way up.

Made it!

It may take a little coaxing. You can use a small treat to encourage your dog to jump. If your dog is resistant or anxious, don't force things. The exercise should be fun!

- Diana Ozimek

Chubby Louie

Tricia Montgomery lost more than 100 pounds. She couldn't have done it without a lovable Basset hound, with extra pounds of his own.

Tricia Montgomery drove up to the park, wiping a bead of sweat from her forehead, trying to chase away the troubling thoughts: No way is anyone going to show up. They're going to think I'm crazy. Why on earth did I ever think this was a good idea? For a moment, she almost considered turning around and heading back home. Who would ever believe that the girl who never met a cookie she didn't like....the girl the neighbor kids had called Fatty Patty... the girl who had been more than 100 pounds overweight....that she, Tricia, was opening a gym. Not just any gym. A gym with a special twist.

Growing up, Tricia faced taunts from other kids because of her weight. Macaroni and cheese, mashed potatoes and gravy, and cookies helped ease the pain, at least for a while. The only other thing

Growing up, Tricia couldn't escape teasing about her weight.

that helped was the love of a faithful dog. Her dog stayed by her side when health problems took her mom away from the family for months at a time. Her dog gave hugs and kisses when a caretaker became abusive. And her dog cuddled close when Tricia's father scolded and punished Tricia because of her weight.

Sometimes, Tricia wasn't sure she was worthy of being loved. But her dog always loved her, no matter what. Her dog never judged her. Her dog didn't care how much she weighed.

As an adult, Tricia's best friend was her Basset hound, Louie. They did everything together. Including gaining weight.

88

Tricia and Louie didn't have many friends. The comfort of friendship was found in food and each other. Tricia thought she was showing love by giving Louie a bit of her food, a slice of pizza, or a piece of bacon. "At least I'm not eating the whole thing," Tricia would say. "This will make us feel better."

He'd gobble it up, showing his appreciation with a wagging tail and affectionate snuggle.

Louie waddled when he walked, although he never had to walk too far. Tricia and Louie spent their time relaxing together, reading, and watching television. Exercise wasn't a part of their routine. Before long, her weight ballooned to 265 pounds.

One day Louie had to go to the vet for his regular checkup. Tricia respected their veterinarian, who had always been kind to them. This time, however, the doctor looked her in the eye, his expression serious. "Louie needs to lose weight," he said. Then he told her, in no uncertain terms, that they were both too fat.

The words shocked Tricia. But once she got over the hurt, the words also motivated her. She hugged Louie tight. "I'll change," she promised. "I'll do it for you."

Tricia set about improving their diet. She chose healthier meals and cut back on portion sizes, and provided Louie with the proper amount of quality dog food. No more table scraps. One afternoon she thought about how great a big bowl of pasta would taste. Louie jumped right up and looked at her with those big Basset eyes as if to say, "You don't need fattening food. You've got me and I've got you!"

But to lose enough weight and get fit, she knew that they had to add exercise. And that was something that hadn't happened in… well, forever.

After work in radio sales, Tricia was too tired to even think about exercising. On Saturday, she woke up and looked outside--a beautiful sunny day. Her vet had mentioned getting Louie outside for walks. But Tricia shrunk back from the window. Taunts from the kids on her block rang in her ears. "Look! Here comes Fatty Patty! Fatty Patty and her fat dog!"

She would not put her—and Louie—up for humiliation like that again. She waited all day, until the sun set. Then, under the cover of darkness, she clipped on Louie's leash and they stepped outside for a walk.

That night they huffed and puffed around the block. Tricia was exhausted. But it felt good to be doing something positive. The next night they went out again. And the next. Her legs ached and her lungs burned. But she kept on walking, farther and farther each night. She looked at Louie. His stubby little legs struggled to keep up. "Atta boy Louie! We got this!" she said. He pranced along, his big ears flopping.

Gradually the weight started coming off, like shedding layers of heavy, suffocating winter clothing. The following weekend Tricia had plans in the evening. But Louie needed his walk. She clipped his leash to his collar and took a deep breath before heading out into the daylight. They made their way to the park. Louie's tail wagged. He seemed to enjoy being out in the sun with all the sights and sounds. People of all ages and sizes walked in the park. Not just beautiful people. Soon, they were walking around the track at the school.

After eleven months of dieting and exercise, Tricia lost 135 pounds, and the vet deemed Louie fit and healthy. They kept up walking. Then the Chicago winter hit. Tricia considered exercising in a gym. But what about Louie? She thought, "If only Louie could come to the gym with me."

At the time, Tricia was working at a new job as the Public Education Director of the Chicago Veterinary Medical Association. She met many people who were devoted to pet health, including pet obesity. These people understood the correlation between human and canine health. Ever since she and Louie lost weight, she wanted to help others do the same. She had a dream—to open a gym where people and dogs could exercise together.

Through hard work and help from pet health professionals, her dream became a reality. She opened a gym for dogs and people to work out together! But she still doubted that anyone would really come. That's when she drove up to the park for the very first class of K9 Fit Club, her stomach in knots.

As she stepped out and looked around, however, she could barely believe what she saw—there, covering the expanse of green designated for the class, were 23 men and women and their dogs, ready and waiting! They were others who knew—as she did—that they'd be more motivated with their best friend involved.

The first K9 Fit Club opened in 2012 in Hinsdale Illinois. From the park, they moved to a church basement, and eventually their own facility. Now there are K9 Fit Communities and Clubs in 31 locations throughout the United States, and growing every day!

Fit and strong, Tricia Montgomery with Zeus.

WOOF WORKOUTS

Your dog is your best friend and your best workout partner. Your dog will never cancel on you and is always happy to exercise. And, exercising is just more fun with your dog by your side! Working out with your dog will help you become a consistent exerciser and your dog will benefit just as much as you do. Active dogs at a healthy weight will avoid many health issues and diseases. Regular exercise for your dog will also help curb anxiety and negative behavior.

Try these exercises to help you lose weight and increase your muscle tone. Have your dog try them with you so they can be healthy and happy too.

Woof Workouts at K9 Fit Club

Exercises designed by K9 Fit Club.
Featuring fitness trainer Diana Ozimek,
Zoe the German Shepherd, and Cleo the Chihuahua.

PLAY TAG

Start by getting your dog's attention.

This is a warm-up drill. It will get your dog focused on what you are doing and ready to follow your lead.

Step 1: Start by getting your dog's attention.

Step 2: Walk forward, keeping your dog in the heel position, with your dog's ear next to your leg. If your dog wants to pull forward, say, "Heel," turn to the right, and continue walking.

Step 3: When you reach a designated spot (cone, tree, end of the room), have your dog turn and face you as you say "Come" and jog backward to starting point. Your dog should follow directly in front of you (facing each other) and shouldn't pass you. This helps your dog work on staying engaged and keeping eye contact with you.

Step 4: Once at the starting point, repeat.

Jog backwards with your dog facing you.

*Remember, "Heel" is only used when you want your dog to move beside you in heel position, with your dog's ear next to your leg. Use "Come" in any other position, so your dog knows to follow you instead of standing next to you.

SIT AND STAY
SIDE LUNGES

Right lunge

Step 1: Have your dog stand facing you.

Step 2: Keeping your left leg straight, step out to the side with your right leg, bending your right knee.

Step 3: Holding the lunge, ask your dog to walk a few steps toward you.

Left lunge

Step 4: Step back to the center, legs together.

Step 5: Do the same exercise on the left side.

Step 6: Repeat 10 times on each side. Remember, your dog should walk side to side as you lunge.

> Your dog doesn't know what you're expecting,
> so be patient when teaching new moves.

PUPPY PLANKS
& PUSH-UPS

Hold the leash in both hands.

Step 1: Ask your dog to sit or lay down next to you.

Step 2: Move into the push-up position. Make sure you have the leash held in both hands.

Step 3: Perform 10 push-ups, keeping your head up and in line with your spine and your abs pulled tight.

Zoe practices her down as Diana completes her push-ups.

Step 4: Now it's time for you pup to do push-ups! Ask your dog to move from a sit to a down, 3 to 5 times.

Zoe sits to begin her puppy push-up.

Zoe moves from a sit into the down position.

The finished position, Zoe has moved from her sit to a down-stay.

Remember to give lots of praise!

WAGGIN' WALL SIT

Step 1: Ask your dog to sit beside you.

Step 2: Place your back against the wall and slide down until your thighs are parallel with the floor. Squeeze your glutes and abs as you press into the wall and hold.

Zoe practices focus and obedience.

Step 3: Ready to take it up a notch? If you have a large dog and you are ready for a challenge, ask your dog to put their front paws in your lap. This adds a decent amount of weight to your hold so be ready for it.

Zoe adds resistance to the exercise.

Step 4: If you have a small dog, hold your dog in your lap for extra resistance. Give your dog lots of hugs while you feel your legs burn!

Cleo is happy to help!

LUCKY DOG
STEPOVERS

You can cover the step with a mat if your dog prefers.

Adding cardio intervals between strength exercises is a great way to increase your caloric burn.

Step 1: Place an exercise step in the middle of the room. If your dog isn't comfortable with the feeling of the plastic step, or if it is slippery for them, cover the step with an exercise mat as shown in the picture. Be sure the mat doesn't slip as you move!

Step 2: With your dog at your side, walk or jog across the room, going up and over the step on your way to the other side.

Step 3: Repeat back and forth for 1-2 minutes.

Step 4: Ready to take it up a notch? Add intensity by adding multiple steps across the room.

Cardio with your dog gets your heart pumping.

When you are done, give your dog a big rubdown from head to tail, and some light stretching for you, too!

Advanced

Exercises

WIGGLE WAGGLE WEAVES

Your dog should watch for your signals.

Step 1: Stand with your dog next to you.

A small treat will help encourage your dog.

Step 2: Lunge one leg forward as you drop your back knee toward the ground.

Step 3: Hold the lunge.

Step 4: Ask your dog to walk under your leg to the other side.

Use a hand signal such as snapping your fingers in the spot where you would like your dog to walk. Use a small treat or favorite toy in your hand to help encourage your dog to walk under and through.

Step 5: After your dog has walked under, pass the leash through to your other hand.

Step 6: Step forward with your back leg so you are now standing.

Step 7: Now lunge forward with your opposite leg, asking your dog to walk under again, moving back to your other side.

Keep lunging as your dog weaves.

This exercise is fun to do together and your legs will get extra work as you hold the lunge while teaching your dog to go under!

POOCH & PEEP
PUSH-UPS

Try this with small dogs only! Do not attempt with a medium or large dog.

This is an advanced exercise for you and your dog. This exercise is more difficult for both partners than it looks. You will either need to teach your dog to jump onto your back or have a partner who can place your small dog on your back.

Push-ups need to be done slowly and with control, while your dog has to work hard to adjust his or her weight and keep balanced as you move up and down.

Step 1: Get into push-up position.

Step 2: Have your dog jump onto your back, or have a partner place the dog on your back.

112

Step 3: Once your dog is in place, slowly begin your push-up. Be sure to keep your abs tight, breathing in on the way down. Keep your body in line and balanced so your dog doesn't go off to one side.

Step 4: Complete your push-up, blowing air out on the way up.

Step 5: Pause at the top of the push-up if you feel your dog needs a second to adjust their stance and balance.

Step 6: Once you complete as many reps as you can, go all the way down to the floor so your dog can safely jump down.

Perform the move slowly! You don't want any doggy motion sickness.

TAIL WAGGING TWIST

Small dogs can add resistance to your workout.

A workout with a fun twist.

Step 1: Hold your dog so your dog is comfortable and feels supported under the hind quarters.

Step 2: With your knees bent and heels on floor, lean back slightly until you are holding yourself tight with your abdominals.

Step 3: Slowly twist from right to left while holding your dog. Be sure you are twisting at the waist and not just moving your dog back and forth.

Hold your dog securely.

Twist from the waist.

 *YOU*

Strength Training

Steve Pelletier is committed to physical fitness. Strength and resistance training is one way to take your workouts to the next level.

Steve practices his pull-ups.

Strength and resistance training is an important part of any exercise program. Whether you are a couch potato, a runner, a yogi, or a weekend athlete, you would be wise to incorporate some form of resistance training in your exercise routines.

Benefits of Strength Training:
- Helps reduce occurrences of health ailments including arthritis, diabetes, and back pain.
- Strengthens the muscular and skeletal systems as well as connective tissues (tendons) which can help prevent injury.
- Helps burn calories and increases your metabolic rate.
- Makes you look and feel great.

Getting Started

If you have never consistently strength trained and want to try it out, good for you! Although it may seem intimidating, there are some simple ways to ease into a smart strength training program without feeling intimidated.

- Get a physical exam and talk with your doctor about your overall health and fitness. If you have any injuries or limitations you will need to take these into account when designing your workout programs (e.g. if you have a bad shoulder, you might avoid overhead pressing movements).
- Strength training does not necessarily mean lifting heavy weights! There are a variety of choices besides barbells including dumbbells and kettlebells, body weight exercises, Pilates, and more. Try as many as you can, and stick with the ones that you find most enjoyable.
- Get some basic training. One of the biggest causes of injuries is poor technique or ill-advised programs. Find an expert trainer (or trainers if you are exploring multiple disciplines like weights and Pilates for example), and learn proper technique, body position-ing, exercise substitutions, and how to construct a safe program. This will be time and money well spent.

Keeping it Going

Progression should be slow and steady. Work out hard, but don't overdo it. You must use common sense and don't fall prey to the old mantra "no pain, no gain."

- Progression is key—to a point. With any kind of training, and strength training in particular, improvements to strength, conditioning, and body appearance are a direct result of using progressively challenging resistance or intensity. If you do the same exercises for the same reps with the same weights, you will make little progress over time and likely get frustrated and quit. Instead, learn to safely push yourself to lift more/more reps/less rest, etc. so that your body is forced to adapt and improve. Lifting to failure (lifting to a point where your muscles cannot properly perform the task) can cause injury and mental burnout, both of which will sabotage your progress.
- Create a balanced program. I recommend that beginners use primarily full body exercises (squats, pushups and pull-ups, kettlebell swings) that work multiple muscle groups at the same time instead of isolation moves (such as curls and most machine exercises). Include unilateral moves (such as dumbbells and one-legged variations) and core and balance exercises to make sure that your build functional strength that you will be able to use in your everyday life—not just when you are in the gym. You want to be able to "go" as well as "show." Of course, if you are working around injuries, machines and isolation exercises can be your only options.
- Learn from your experience and adjust. There is no such thing as a single best approach to strength training. Try different exercises and set/rep formats for 4-6 weeks and see which your body best responds to and which ones you enjoy the most. Make sure to work out hard. Be honest about it and you will see great progress. Making progress, feeling better, and having fun are the easiest ways to ensure that strength training will become a part of your lifestyle ...forever.

- Steve Pelletier

Strength and Resistance Training Equipment

dumbbells

kettle weights

medicine balls

resistance bands

ankle weights

weighted vests

home gyms

A home gym can be anything from simple to extravagant.

 **YOUR DOG**

Strength Training

Jack sports his very own weighted vest.

The Weighted Vest for Dogs

As an athlete, I have used a weighted vest for many years to increase the intensity level of my exercise drills. In addition to building muscle and stamina, the extra intensity can help with EPO (Excess Post Exercise Oxygen Consumption), or burning extra calories after the workout is completed. As often is the case, what works for humans can work for dogs!

My yellow lab Jack is a fan of resistance training. In the beginning, I often placed a backpack on Jack, filled with water bottles for extra weight, so he would burn more energy and calories and also build some muscle to replace his fat. The pack worked well for walks but was not usable for runs or any other fast-paced exercise drills because the weight was not evenly distributed and the pack would often shift when he moved quickly.

Now I use a weighted vest for dogs, much like my own vest. Jack's weighted vest adds resistance to several different drills including stairs, sprints, and change of direction drills. Jack loves it and he is completely exhausted when we are done, even though our workouts last only 12-15 minutes! Talk about efficiency—using a vest can be a great tool for those pressed for time.

Benefits of using a weighted vest while exercising:
- Higher caloric burn for the same exercise.[xxv] The more intense the exercise and the heavier the vest, the greater the increased caloric expenditures.
- Faster weight loss.[xxvi]
- Build/maintain muscle. More muscle adds greater protection for your dog's joints and skeletal system (the same is true for humans).
- Work off energy. As with any challenging workout, the physical activity is a positive outlet for pent-up energy that might otherwise be misdirected.

Partner workout.

Getting Started
Whenever you start a new exercise program for your dog, you should first consult with your veterinarian to make sure that there are

no health issues that might restrict activity. Once cleared to exercise, follow these tips to safely introduce strength training into your dog's exercise regimen:

- Start slowly. Ease into the new program slowly, adding a few minutes of resistance training per session each week. Start by using the vest on short walks.
- Don't overload your dog. Keep the added resistance to less than 5% of the dog's bodyweight. Adding too much weight can cause form problems and potentially lead to injuries.
- Keep a close eye on how your dog reacts to the vest. If she appears uncomfortable, you may have the wrong size. Also, you don't want the vest (or the weight packs) to shift much. If you notice this it means that the vest is too big or improperly adjusted.

Keeping it Going

- Remember that with added resistance comes added intensity. Work your way up, but keep resistance sessions reasonable. I recommend no more than 30 minutes for most dogs.
- Progress from walks to short runs.
- When your dog is ready, use the weighted vest for more intense drills and activities.

- Steve Pelletier

Jack checks out the kettlebell.

122

Maintenance

 # YOU

Tips for Maintaining Weight Loss

Most of us who have lost weight know how easy it is to gain everything back, often even more. Maintaining weight loss can be challenging. Here are some tips to help.

If you need to get your head back in the game:

- Celebrate successes--you deserve it!

- **Celebrate holidays, birthdays, and events in ways other than eating.**

- Find a different type of exercise--you may have become bored with yours.

- **Don't compare your progress to others. This can be a real diet saboteur.**

- Stop making excuses--too tired, too busy, it's raining outside. Instead, plan how to succeed.

- **Eliminate stress, which may contribute to overeating.**

- Make a list of obstacles and roadblocks. Explore ways to handle them.

- **Reaffirm your commitment to losing weight. One of the best reasons is keeping yourself and your dog healthy!**

Kelly and Peggy work on maintaining their weight loss.

If you've noticed you've gained a few:

- Keep weighing-in regularly--daily, weekly, or whatever works for you. This helps maintain a focus on your weight.

- **Dig out your food journal and commit to writing down everything you eat for at least a week. Analyze the list and look for trends and trouble spots.**

- Measure your food. Your portion sizes may be slipping.

- **Increase the time spent or intensity of your exercise.**

- Don't skip meals, particularly breakfast. Studies show that eating a healthy breakfast helps in an overall weight-loss program.

- **Plan ahead for holidays and parties so that you don't overeat.**

- Restock your fridge with healthy food and snacks.

- **Consider joining a weight-loss group for support.**

125

 # YOUR DOG

Tips for Maintaining Weight Loss

If your dog is starting to gain weight:

- Schedule a checkup with the vet to make sure there are no new underlying health problems.

- **Weigh your dog regularly to keep a focus on progress.**

- Increase your dog's exercise duration and intensity.

- **Take a look at your dog's food and evaluate if you need to switch to a higher quality food.**

- Make sure you are still measuring your dog's food at each feeding.

- **Your dog shouldn't feel hungry between meals. Review the healthy snacks list. Pumpkin, for example, helps your dog feel full.**

- Are you rewarding your dog with food again? Show your love in hugs and play.

- **Consider adding a new activity or sport to your dog's routine!**

Keeping those Doggone Pounds Off

Patti Lawson is an award-winning author who writes about dogs, and in particular her dog, Sadie. She lives in West Virginia, is an attorney, and supports all causes that make the lives of animals better.

Sadie helps Patti create a salad box with fresh vegetables.

The story of how I lost 30 pounds after adopting my dog Sadie became my first book. A skinny me and my trim dog went from city to city signing books, giving talks, making new friends, and meeting wonderful dogs. We were always surprised with gift baskets in our very nice hotel rooms. From New York to Miami, we were on a magical book tour having the time of our lives. When it was time to get off the gravy train, both Sadie and I regretted that we'd eaten so many mashed potatoes.

It's not easy to stay in shape for dogs or people. As a Dog Mom, I control what and when Sadie eats. The problem is, my own indulgences transfer to her. A bite here, a treat to satisfy her while I eat something she can't…the calories and the pounds add up. We've discovered ways to keep our weight at a healthy level while not depriving ourselves of things we enjoy.

Patti and Sadie motivate each other.

1. Don't buy it and you won't eat it. The grocery store and the pet store are where your maintenance program begins. Don't bring home chips, cookies, and other empty nutrition snacks. Fill your refrigerator with fresh organic fruit, vegetables, and natural cheese for snacking. Buy your dog high quality natural treats.

2. Make exercise a non-negotiable part of your daily routine and adjust times during extreme temperatures. Raining? No problem. Sadie has a rain coat, I have an umbrella. Get up just 30 minutes earlier and both you and your dog will enjoy a more energized day. Sadie gets two 15 minute playtimes at school (daycare) and I take a 20 minute walk at work when my schedule permits. We do an evening walk plus play time in the yard. Sadie does get to watch TV when I work out.

3. Set regular meal times. Sadie and I eat breakfast within an hour of getting up. Our evening meal is always before 8:00 p.m. She gets one treat when she comes in from the last "pester" and I get one square of dark chocolate. During the day I have a mid-morning snack of yogurt, fruit or nuts, and a healthy lunch.

4. Weigh yourself weekly. Clothes are the great reminder of what is happening to your body, but that number on the scale will keep you aware of how you're doing with your food choices. I check Sadie with the "healthy hug" method.(You can find how to do this with a quick Google search.)

5. RELAX. Food is a wonderful part of life. If you want something, have it. Don't pass up the chance for dinner at a special restaurant. Make wise choices and cut back somewhere else. Exercise more. Let you dog have that extra treat for something extraordinary…which can be just for being herself.

- Patti Lawson

YOUR DOG 🐾

Fit Tips

- If you are hot, your dog is hotter. Take into consideration your dog is exercising in a fur coat. Provide lots of water, stay in the shade on sunny days, and exercise early in the morning and later in the evening.

- Weekend warriors do not equal a fit person or dog. Both of you need exercise on a consistent basis.

- If your dog is not used to exercise, treat your dog like a beginner. Introduce your dog to exercises slowly with short sessions a few times per week. Increase the duration and frequency slowly as your dog becomes more fit.

- Allow a couple of hours between feeding and exercise. If that's not possible, give your dog a partial meal before the workout and the rest of the meal after your dog has had some recovery time.

- Keep your dog's paws safe. Pads on a dog's paw can be injured by hot surfaces, cold surfaces, hard surfaces, sand, trash, broken glass, and more. Be sure to check your dog's paws before and after every workout. When needed, use a safe and secure paw cover or boot for your dog.

- If you are feeling sore from your exercise routine, your dog may be feeling sore too. Find a massage therapist and a dog massage therapist and book relaxing massages for both of you.

- Be patient and have fun! Changing from a casual walk to an exercise plan may be confusing for your dog. One day your dog is allowed to sniff the grass and the next you are asking your dog to pay attention and work with you. Be consistent in your training and your dog will understand when it's time to be your workout partner.

Giant Breeds
- Giant breeds such as Mastiffs need exercise to keep them at a healthy weight. Give giant breeds moderate exercise, and avoid sustained running on hard surfaces.

- Keep giant breeds' exercise low-impact; do not have them repeatedly jump on and off benches around the park.

- Be aware that giant breeds are more likely than other breeds to suffer hip dysplasia and arthritis. Giant puppies under 1 year are prone to stress fractures and breaks.

Puppies
- Puppies should be kept on low-impact exercise until they are done growing so as not to cause stress fractures or other issues. Small dogs mature faster, while giant breeds may take up to 2 years to mature. Most medium to large breeds are still growing until they are about 18 months old.

- Puppies' attention spans are short. Exercise a few times a day for 10-15 minutes. Keep training interesting and end on a good note before they become bored and distracted.

- Sustained running should not be done with dogs that are not yet fully grown, causing extra stress on bones, joints and ligaments. Check with your veterinarian on a good age to start jogging with your breed of dog.

Short-nosed Breeds
- Short-nosed breeds have difficulty breathing with increased activity. When working with short-nosed breeds, such as pugs and bulldogs, keep the exercise light with multiple rest periods.

Senior Dogs
- Have a checkup with your vet if you are starting a senior dog on an exercise routine.

- Take care with your environment. Senior dogs have a more difficult time regulating their body temperature, and are sensitive to heat and humidity.

- Let your senior dog take the lead. Your dog's activity level will change as your dog ages. Pay attention to how your dog is feeling and reacting. Easy, short walks a couple of times per day may be enough.

  - Diana Ozimek

YOUR DOG

Five Signs your Dog is Fit

1. Your dog can comfortably finish the workout without undue stress or fatigue (e.g. collapsing or taking long rest breaks).
2. Your dog's exercise does not impact their ability to do other normal dog things during the rest of the day. While they may take a post-workout nap, they remain energetic throughout the day and are up for a game of fetch or tug or whatever else they usually enjoy.
3. Your dog exhibits "happy behavior," which is a general appearance of being happy, satisfied, and curious. With high intensity exercise, your dog may even experience something akin to the "runner's high" that humans experience.
4. Your dog's muscle tone is well defined and their waist is visible and tapered.
5. Your dog's coat is full, thick and shiny and they have a healthy appetite.

   - Steve Pelletier

Hudson the yellow Lab gets fit swimming in the lake.

*YOU*

Motivation

- List all the ways keeping yourself healthy will benefit you and your dog.

- Practice positive affirmations, such as "I'm getting stronger and fitter every day."

- Join a weight loss support group.

- Be selfish—it's okay to put yourself first when it comes to your health.

- Remember you are in control of your life and your health. You can do it!

- If you take medication that might be reduced or discarded by losing weight, set a goal of working toward getting off your medication.

- Enjoy the increased energy you are starting to feel, or hope to feel, by losing weight.

- Keep on growing, learning, and pushing yourself.

- Meditate, pray.

- Reward yourself for your accomplishments along the way.

 *YOU*

Motivational Quotes

"Strive for progress, not perfection." –Unknown

"You miss 100% of the shots you don't take." –Wayne Gretzky

"Strength does not come from physical capacity. It comes from an indomitable will." –Mahatma Gandhi

"Energy and persistence conquer all things." –Benjamin Franklin

"Insanity is doing the same thing over and over again and expecting different results." –Albert Einstein

"Physical fitness is not only one of the most important keys to a healthy body; it is the basis of dynamic and creative intellectual activity." –John F. Kennedy

"The difference between try and triumph is just a little umph!" –Marvin Phillips

"Look to your health; and if you have it, praise God and value it next to conscience; for health is the second blessing that we mortals are capable of, a blessing money can't buy." –Izaak Walton

"Average effort yields average results." –Unknown

"Our health always seems much more valuable after we lose it." –Unknown

"The good Lord gave you a body that can stand most anything. It's your mind you have to convince." –Vincent Lombardi

Resources

Health/Wellness:

American Diabetes Association

http://www.diabetes.org/food-and-fitness/fitness/weight-loss/

American Heart Association http://www.heart.org

American Medical Association http://www.ama-assn.org/ama

American Veterinary Medical Association https://www.avma.org

Association for Pet Obesity Prevention

http://www.petobesityprevention.com/

National Heart, Lung, and Blood Institute (NHLBI)

www.nhlbi.nih.gov

Pet MD http://www.petmd.com

SPCA http://www.Spca.org/petobesity

Stop Canine Obesity http://stopcanineobesity.com

Exercise:

Bark for Life

http://www.relayforlife.org/learn/relayforeveryone/barkforlife

Cool running http://www.coolrunning.com

Couch to 5k http://www.coolrunning.com/engine/2/2_3/181.shtml

Dog Treadmills http://dogtread.com/

K9 Fit Club www.k9fitclub.com

K9 Kamp http://peggyfrezon.blogspot.com/p/k9-kamp.html

Physical activity guidelines www.health.gov/paguidelines

Pooch to 5k http://www.poochto5k.com/

Slimdoggy www.slimdoggy.com

American Kennel Club http://www.akc.org

United States Dog Agility Association http://usdaa.com/events.cfm

Food/diet (You):

Dietary Guidelines for Americans www.dietaryguidelines.gov

Dieting with my Dog http://peggyfrezon.com

Food Journal Web MD

http://www.webmd.com/diet/printable/food-fitness-journal

Nutrition Facts label information

www.cfsan.fda.gov/~dms/foodlab.html

USDA My Plate http://www.choosemyplate.gov/

USDA Calorie Supertracker

https://www.supertracker.usda.gov/default.aspx

Food/diet (Your Dog):

Dog Food Advisor http://www.dogfoodadvisor.com

Dog food recipes http://kolchakpuggle.com

Dog food reviews http://www.dogfoodreviews.net/

Calculators:

BMI calculator http://www.webmd.com/diet/calc-bmi-plus

Body type calculator

http://www.calculator.net/body-type-calculator.html

Calories burned in a workout calculator:

http://www.coolrunning.com/engine/4/4_1/94.shtml

Calories in food calculator

https://www.supertracker.usda.gov/foodapedia.aspx

Fat and sodium calculator

http://www.heart.org/fatsandsodiumexplorer/explorer.html

Heart Attack Risk Calculator

https://www.heart.org/gglRisk/main_en_US.html

Ideal weight calculator

http://www.calculator.net/ideal-weight-calculator.html

K9 Fit Club. Fitness & Dogs = Pawsitive Rewards.

K9 Fit Club is growing a nationwide community of clubs dedicated to the health and wellness of dogs and people, founded and created by Tricia Montgomery in 2008.

According to the Centers for Disease Control and Prevention (CDC), two out of every three US adults are overweight or obese. Over half our country's dogs are too heavy by veterinary standards in a 2012 nationwide survey and only 1.2% of Americans met the seven cardiovascular health habits recommended by the American Heart Association (AHA) in a 2012 Journal of the American Medical Association study.

K9 Fit Club combines fitness with friendship of man's best friend – their dog. The best way to stick with a workout program is having a workout partner. A dog is the best workout partner you can ask for, always excited to go, will never cancel and is always the happiest when by their person's side.

By blending the motivational support of a dog with fitness goals for both person and pooch, a change in mental attitude occurs and improved wellness and health benefits are the result. K9 Fit Club members enjoy cardio, strength and obedience training in a fun environment. Members say hello to weight loss, better fitness and increased stamina and say good-bye to depression, stress, anxiety— and certain misbehaviors in their dogs.

Our programs have been developed with the cooperation of personal trainers, dog trainers and veterinarians to ensure the best quality for both person and dog. K9 Fit Club offers group and individual instruction, both indoors and outdoors, using proprietary programs including: Oh My Dog Bootcamp™, Bow Wow Bootcamp™,

139

Pupilates™, Tai Chi Wa Wa™ and Fungility™. K9 Fit Club's headquarters and training facility are located in Hinsdale, Illinois where we have on-staff and consulting veterinarians, doctors, certified animal behaviorists, people and pup personal trainers passionate about developing human/animal bonding programs.

K9 Fit Club's programs are customized to individual fitness and goals of both dog and owner. Each pup and person undergoes an evaluation that includes cardiovascular endurance, muscular endurance, obedience assessment, nutritional assessment, behavior and activity analysis and more. K9 Fit Club also has specialty programs for breast cancer survivors, those with Down syndrome, hearing impairment, and spina bifida.

K9 Fit Club proves that Working Out is Not So Ruff™ with classes guaranteed to eliminate boredom, keep you and your dog pawsitive, build your confidence and on your way to a New Leash on Life™

If you are interested in opening your K9 Fit Club, please contact K9 Fit Club info@K9Fitclub.com or call 630/920-1476. We are Changing Lives One Dog at a Time™.

Club Locations (as of August 2013):

Hinsdale, IL
Westmont, IL
Chicago, IL
Winnetka, CA
Raleigh/Durham, NC
Cary, NC
Chapel Hill, NC
New York, NY
Chesterfield, MO

St. Charles, MO
Washington DC
Del Ray, FL
Tampa, FL
Memphis, TN
Atlanta, GA
Rochester, NY
Portland, OR
Reading, PA

slimdoggy

SlimDoggy grew out of our experience with Jack, an overweight yellow Labrador that we rescued in August 2011. Little did we know that there are a lot of dogs like Jack. According to the Association for Pet Obesity Prevention, there are close to 40 million overweight/obese dogs in the US alone. The incremental cost in vet/medicine bills to address health issues related to obesity is an estimated $6-8 billion per year. We also learned that being overweight shaves years off a dog's life, just as it does with humans.

Based on these startling and disturbing facts, we decided to create an App based our successful work with Jack and attack the dog obesity problem head on. Features of the App include:

1. Ability to research dog foods in our database of 2,000 foods. We provide calorie counts, ingredients and a quality score you can select the right foods and the right portion for your dog.
2. Enter your dog's daily activities and we calculate the calories they expend.
3. The App's Diary combines food calories and exercise and you can see exactly how many calories your dog needs each day and adjust their food or exercise appropriately.

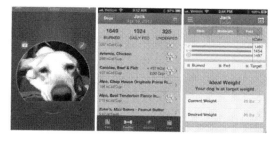

Slimdoggy App is available in the iTunes App store.

Follow the blog, where we write about dog fitness & health. You will find lots of good tips and advice for keeping your dog healthy & fit.

Slimdoggy: http://slimdoggy.com
Twitter: @MySlimDoggy
FaceBook: SlimDoggy

Biographies

Steve Pelletier

Steve Pelletier is an experienced technology and start-up executive with a passion for health and fitness for people and pets. He is the founder of SlimDoggy, which provides tools and tips to dog owners to help their dog achieve and maintain a healthy weight and a healthy and happy life. Prior to that, he was SVP for LibreezeFitness, a curated directory of "the best of the web" health and fitness content. Pelletier was also the founder and former CEO of FatTail, the premier provider of contract and inventory management, workflow, and reporting software for online publishers.

Steve and his family are active contributors to several LA area dog rescues. He and his wife currently share their home with Jack and Maggie, two Labrador rescues who never cease to make them smile.

Tricia Montgomery
President and Founder of K9 Fit Club

Tricia has merged her career in the veterinary profession, her passion for pets and their people along with her personal journey of weight loss into a program that Changes Lives One Dog at a Time. No matter how large, how small, the breed or mix, K9 Fit Club has something for everyone.

As the former Executive Director/Public Education Director for the Chicago Veterinary Medical Association, Public Relations for the International Kennel Club Show, Tricia has also worked with the AVMA, AAHA and HSUS. K9 Fit Club is based on her personal story of working out and losing over 130 lbs. with her dog.

Diana Ozimek
Fitness trainer

I have been very lucky to be able to combine my career in fitness with my love for dogs. I have been in the fitness industry for more than 15 years working as a personal trainer, group instructor, Director of Trainers as well as owning and instructing my own boot camp, Windy City Adventure Boot Camp, since 2007. Throughout that time I have volunteered for different rescue groups in many ways; as a foster home, in shelters, running programs for shelter dogs and organizing pet adoption events. I currently volunteer with Safe Humane Chicago's Court Case Dog program.

I have been lucky enough to have two amazing workout partners; my first running partner, Chandler, and my dog Zoe who helped me develop a popular and innovative fitness program for both dogs and their owners. I hope many people and their dogs will enjoy the benefits and fun of being workout partners.

144

Contributors

Rosalyn Acero and Sugar, Sugar the Golden Retriever
http://www.sugarthegoldenretriever.com

Sarah Burdo, Charlie and Homie

Michele Cuke

Patti Lawson and Sadie http://www.thedogdiet.com
http://redroom.com/member/patti-lawson
http://blogs.dailymail.com/petcity

Steve Pelletier, Slimdoggy http://slimdoggy.com

Jessica Rhae, Chester and Gretel, You Did What With Your Weiner
http://youdidwhatwithyourweiner.com

Kate Richards and Scooter, Paws and Pedals
http://www.actiondog.com.au

Donna B. Russell and Paige, Petwise Online
http://petwiseonline.blogspot.com

Diana Silver and Rocco, To Dog With Love
http://www.todogwithlove.com

Annette Vivian and Snoopy, Snoopy's Dog Blog
http://snoopysdogblog.com/

Krista Wickens, Dog Tread- http://DogTread.com/blog

Other Books by Peggy Frezon

Paperback • 17x22cm • 112 pages • 25 color pictures
HH4406 • ISBN: 978-1-845844-06-6 • UPC: 6-36847-04406-0

Dieting With My Dog; One busy life, two full figures...and unconditional love is the honest and heartfelt story of one overweight woman and her chubby spaniel, struggling to lose weight and get fit together. This book is for anyone who has ever loved a pet – through thick and thin.

Published by Hubble and Hattie http://www.hubbleandhattie.com

Amazon: http://www.amazon.com/Dieting-With-My-Dog-Unconditional/dp/1845844068/

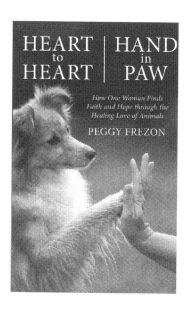

Paperback • 5.9x8.9cm • 170 pages • color pictures
IV • ISBN: 978-1462400775• UPC: 9-781462-40077-5

Heart to Heart, Hand in Paw

Luanne and her husband share a dream of living a simple life in the beautiful Vermont countryside. But--
• the dog has separation anxiety.
• the goose is afraid of water.
• there's a fox in the pigpen and raccoons in the hen house.
• the homesick donkey cries all night.
• the truck has slipped into the pond.
And from there, things only get worse!
Drawing upon a lifetime of meaningful relationships with animals, Luanne finds the courage to persevere, and discovers strength in a most surprising place. A true tale of faith and the healing bonds of animals.

Inspiring Voices http://www.inspiringvoices.com/

Amazon: http://www.amazon.com/Heart-Hand-Paw-Through-Healing/dp/1462400779/

Coming Soon

The Dieting with my Dog Cookbook

January 2014

About the Author

Peggy Frezon is the author of *Heart to Heart, Hand in Paw, Dieting with My Dog*, and the forthcoming *Dieting with my Dog Cookbook*. She's editor at *Be the Change for Animals*, writes for *Guideposts* magazine and *Angels on Earth*, and is a regular contributor to *Chicken Soup for the Soul* books. Connect with her at Peggy's Pet Place:
www.peggyfrezon.blogspot.com
Newsletter *Pawsitively Pets:*
http://peggyfrezon.blogspot.com/p/pawsitively-pets.html
Website: http://peggyfrezon.com
Peggy Frezon, Author on Facebook:
https://www.facebook.com/PeggyFrezonBooks
Twitter @peggyfrezon

149

Acknowledgements

Special thanks to Jude Brooks and Hubble and Hattie for publishing *Dieting with my Dog; One busy life, two full figures...and unconditional love*, and for granting permissions for *The Dieting with my Dog Guide to Weight Loss and Maintenance*. Thank you to Mike who supports me in everything from writing to working out, dieting to dog parenting (and so much more). To Kate, without whom I'm pretty sure I'd be using my laptop only as a paperweight. To Tricia Montgomery and Zeus at K9 Fit Club, and Diana Ozimek, Zoe and Cleo for all the amazing exercises. To Jodi Chick for being quick to help. And to all the dog bloggers who inspire me with their stories and their dogs.

Appendix

[i] American Heart Association. http://www.heart.org

[ii] Association for Pet Obesity Prevention. http://www.petobesityprevention.com/

[iii] American Heart Association. http://www.heart.org/HEARTORG/GettingHealthy/WeightManagement/Body MassIndex/Body-Mass-Index-BMI-Calculator_UCM_307849_Article.jsp and http://www.surgeongeneral.gov/library/calls/obesity/fact_advice.html

[iv] American Heart Association. http://www.heart.org/HEARTORG/GettingHealthy/NutritionCenter/Body-Composition-Tests_UCM_305883_Article.jsp

[v] Association for Pet Obesity Prevention http://www.petobesityprevention.com/wp-content/uploads/2010/05/DogBCS_APOP.pdf

[vi] Met Life, Halls.md Ideal Weight chart http://www.halls.md/ideal-weight/met.htm

[vii] Association for Pet Obesity Prevention. http://www.petobesityprevention.com/

[viii] U.S. Department of Agriculture http://www.choosemyplate.gov/

[ix] petMD http://www.petmd.com/dog/nutrition/evr_dg_the_best_food_for_dogs?page=2#.Uc3KcW2-Fr0

[x] Association of American Feed Control Officials http://www.aafco.org/

[xi] American Heart Association. http://www.heart.org/HEARTORG/GettingHealthy/WeightManagement/LosingWeight/5-Goals-to-Healthy-Eating_UCM_307257_Article.jsp

[xii] U.S. Department of Agriculture http://www.usda.gov

[xiii] U.S. Department of Agriculture http://www.choosemyplate.gov/food-groups/grains.html

[xiv] The Paleo Diet http://thepaleodiet.com/

[xv] Association of American Feed Control Officials
http://www.petfood.aafco.org/caloriecontent.aspx

[xvi] Association of American Feed Control Officers http://petfood.aafco.org/

[xvii] U.S. Department of Agriculture
http://www.choosemyplate.gov/weight-management-calories/calories/empty-calories-amount.html

[xviii] Association for Pet Obesity Prevention.
http://www.petobesityprevention.com/

[xix] http://www.goredforwomen.org/home/about-heart-disease-in-women/

[xx] American Heart Association. http://www.heart.org

[xxi] American Heart Association. http://www.heart.org

[xxii] American Heart Association. http://www.heart.org

[xxiii] American Heart Association. http://www.heart.org

[xxiv] Cool Running http://www.coolrunning.com/engine/2/2_3/181.shtml

[xxv] "The effect of weighted vest walking on metabolic responses and ground reaction forces." http://www.ncbi.nlm.nih.gov/pubmed/16679992

[xxvi] "A Randomized Trial Comparing the Weight Loss of Canines That Walked With and Without the TrimDog Exercise Belt"
http://www.jarvm.com/articles/Vol9Iss2/Vol9%20Iss2Rohrer.pdf

Made in the USA
Lexington, KY
28 September 2013